FIGHTERS
AND
BOMBERS
OF WORLD WAR II
IN COLOR

FIGHTERS AND BOMBERS
OF WORLD WAR II IN COLOR

MICHAEL J H TAYLOR

Bison Books

First published in 1985 by
Bison Books Ltd
176 Old Brompton Road
London SW5
England

Copyright © 1985 Bison Books Ltd

ISBN 0 86124 224 6

Printed in Hong Kong

Page 1: A staffel of Focke Wulf Fw 190 fighters
line up at their home base.
Page 2-3: Three P-51 Mustangs with the new
teardrop cockpit canopies and an old-style P-51 of
the 375th Fighter Squadron, 8th Air Force, leave
England in finger four formation to escort USAAF
bombers raiding Germany in 1944.
This page: A Bristol Beaufighter takes off from an
airfield in the Western Desert.

CONTENTS

INTRODUCTION

The severe limitations imposed upon Germany regarding the size and type of aircraft allowed to be constructed after the 1914-18 war had, by 1926, virtually been waived as the result of German pressure. A new agreement between Germany and the Allies was signed in Paris on 22 May 1926. Though still forbidding military aviation, it allowed Germany to construct large multi-engined and powerful aircraft for commercial use. By September the Inter-Allied Air Control Commission had withdrawn from Germany, leaving the responsibility of enforcing the new rules to the League of Nations.

Under the 1926 agreement, the German government had to ensure there was no construction, possession or import of aeroplanes or dirigibles equipped with weapons, means of armed protection or armor, and that development of civil flying was within the bounds of normal expansion. Further, the German government had to ensure that imported aircraft which could be construed as racing types conformed to the terms of the agreement. Other regulations covered the training of racing pilots and so on.

Since German manufacturing companies had already flouted the spirit of the 1919 Versailles Treaty by helping to establish production of military aircraft in countries outside Germany, the 1926 Paris agreement was on shaky ground from the start. At the beginning of the year Deutsche Luft Hansa had been founded by the merger of smaller airlines and soon established itself as the world's largest commercial operator. By the winter of 1926-27 several large aircraft were in production, intended for commercial operation but giving the manufacturers the chance of establishing the techniques for any subsequent production of large military machines. Civil flying schools were also expanded and increased in number.

Meanwhile, German personnel and the Soviet Air Fleet had worked together in mid 1926 on a survey of part of Siberia and China, with a view to expanding commercial services to the Far East. Co-operation between Germany and the Soviet Union had a more suspect side, however. Following an agreement between the two nations in 1925, 50 Dutch-built Fokker D XIII single-seat biplane fighters were sent by sea to the Soviet Union where, in 1927, a training air base was established for German military pilots. Similar schools for other forms of warfare were set up at the same time, including those to train Germans in the modern use of tanks and gas.

Gradually the German government issued specifications for new large commercial aircraft and single-seat sporting types which could be easily converted into military machines; indeed, several early passenger, mail and freight transports were actually designed to accept alternative military equipment. By 1933 and the ascension of Hitler's National Socialist Party, the aircraft available for military purposes and the quality of trained pilots were such that it took little time before the existence of the reborn Luftwaffe could be announced to the world. In May 1933 the former Reichs Commission for Aviation became the German Air Ministry under the control of World War I fighter ace Hermann Göring, and training schools in all 15 air districts of Germany were producing many pilots for 'sport flying.'

By 1935, the effects of the 1926 withdrawal of the 'nine rules' were all too apparent: German manufacturers had achieved an output of military aircraft equal to approximately 10 warplanes a day, and the industry was still growing. German aviation might have been nearly strangled by the 1919 Versailles Treaty but a new generation of the world's youth would have to suffer the consequences of international indifference.

Right: A formation of nine Luftwaffe He 111 bombers approach enemy territory. The Heinkel He 111 served throughout the war in many theaters.

The author would like to acknowledge and thank sincerely all the individuals, organizations and companies who assisted in the preparation of this book. In particular, special thanks must go to the aircraft manufacturing companies in several countries that dug deep into their archives to offer statistics and illustrations, and to my fellow author Bill Gunston.

Michael JH Taylor

CHAPTER 1

OVERTURE TO BLITZKRIEG

During the four decades since the end of World War II, many attempts have been made to examine and re-examine the reasons why Germany and Japan could not sustain their early successes in battle and why they eventually capitulated to the Allies. Each facet of equipment, manufacturing support, organisation, training, leadership and the gamut of other considerations has been probed. Rarely is failure found to be lack of courage – and yet so complex is warfare that the true cause of defeat, or more rightly a combination of factors, is virtually impossible to define.

Why Germany's early victories in the air were not repeated wholesale requires greater investigation than Poland's inability to defend itself in September 1939. There are, however, common factors. Six years before the German invasion of Poland, for example, the Lotnictwo Wojskowe (Polish air force) had the world's only first-line fighter force comprising all-metal monoplanes. When war broke out in September 1939 a number of the same fighters (PZL P.7s) remained in service, and those that had passed out of the front line had been replaced only by more powerful derivatives of the same basic design. Likewise, the number of entirely new types of German aircraft deployed by the Luftwaffe in quantity after the Battle of Britain had been fought was surprisingly small, leading to the inescapable conclusion that far too many 1939 warplanes and their derivatives were relied upon for too long. Germany's subsequent mad scramble for new-technology warplanes after the Allies had secured a seemingly unchallengeable upper hand produced only a few types that played any major role in the air war and these were, on the whole, far too late to allow the Luftwaffe a second spell of air superiority.

Historically, World War II began a little after 0430 hours on 1 September 1939 when a small force of Junkers Ju 87B-1s from Stukageschwader 1 (close support group 1) attacked Polish positions around the vital Dirschau railway bridge over the Vistula at Tczew. Such was the importance of this target area that shortly after this action it came under further attack from Dornier Do 17 bombers of III/KG 3. However, even before the Do 17s had pressed home their attack, the first Luftwaffe aircraft to be

Right: Junkers Ju 87B-1s of StG 77 receive their warloads prior to a dive-bombing mission. The type was slow, poorly armed and unmaneuverable, yet gained a fearsome reputation.

destroyed in air-to-air combat during World War II had fallen to the PZL P.11c fighter of Lt Gnys flying in the vicinity of Olkusz.

Although not apparent at the time, the overtures to World War II had really begun in the early 1930s when memories of the 1914-18 war were still vivid. At the time Poland was deploying its P.7s, Germany was in the early stages of forming a clandestine air force in violation of the 1919 Versailles Treaty. Although Germany's build-up of military forces had not gone entirely un-noticed, steps were not taken to prevent that nation from becoming, once again, the most heavily armed in Europe. Indeed, by October 1933 Germany had left the League of Nations and this, coupled with Japan's earlier with-drawal, effectively put an end to the world disarmament talks.

On 26 January 1934 Germany and Poland concluded a non-aggression pact, in which Germany guaranteed to recognise Polish territorial rights for 10 years. By March 1935 Germany felt strong enough to defy the Versailles and Paris treaties openly and announced the existence of the Luftwaffe, in the same month putting all blame for the failure to achieve international disarmament on other countries. It then began a huge mili-tary expansion programme.

Germany's military stance by 1935 was causing great concern to many European nations. France and the Soviet Union con-cluded a pact in May, while another was agreed between the Soviet Union and Czecho-slovakia. In March 1936 German forces re-occupied the Rhineland without opposition, Hitler having renounced the Locarno Treaty pacts dating from the 1920s. The Spanish Civil War that began on 18 July 1936 gave Germany the opportunity to test its air force and equipment under actual battle condi-tions, in support of the Nationalist forces. By doing so it gained important mineral conces-sions that were vital to the continued expan-sion of German forces. By November 1936 German aircraft were in direct conflict with Soviet fighters that had been supplied pre-viously to the Republican forces. But it was the bombing of Guernica, seat of the Basque government in Spain, on 26 April 1937 that really shook the world, proving a more powerful lesson in the capabilities of modern bombing aircraft than any of Italy's actions against the lightly-armed tribesmen of Abyssinia (Ethiopia) during 1935-36.

On another front, Japan began a full-scale invasion of China following a night-time clash at Lukouchiao on 7 July 1937, thereby restarting a war that had been off and on since 18 September 1931. Meanwhile Hitler was, in 1937, planning his *Lebensraum* programme which provided for German ex-pansion into Austria, Czechoslovakia, Poland and the Soviet Union, either by agree-ment or war.

While hopes were still high in 1938 that Europe would not be plunged into another war with Germany, steps were being taken quietly and slowly by a number of countries

Above: *A derivative of the P.11 designed for engines of up to 1000hp was the Polish PZL P.24, examples of which were also acquired by Turkey (as shown), Romania, Bulgaria and Greece. Romanian P.24s were operational on the Eastern Front, while Greek machines (with Gloster Gladiators and Bloch 151s) had the task of staving off the Regia Aeronautica and Luftwaffe.*

Right: *PZL P.11c fighters of the Lotnictwo Wojskowe take off for battle, leaving a P.37B Los B bomber on the airfield.*

to prepare for the worst. Britain's expansion of the shadow factory scheme, for example, allowed for increased aircraft production by non-aviation companies should the need arise. In July of that year fighting began between Japanese and Soviet forces over a wide area.

September 1938 marked the beginning of the slide towards war. On 10 September Germany introduced air corridors from which foreign civil aircraft flying over German airspace were not allowed to leave, thus ensuring its military activities were kept secret. The brewing crisis over Germany's claim to the Sudetenland of Czechoslovakia was also coming to a head in September, with Britain's Prime Minister, Neville Chamberlain, flying to Germany on more than one occasion to prevent the issue from beginning a European war. On the 24th Czech forces were mobilised in anticipation of a German invasion. Since Britain and France were militarily too weak to prevent German forces from invading Czechoslovakia, the Munich crisis was resolved by giving Germany *carte blanche* to occupy the Sudetenland. Had Britain and France been strong enough to stand against Germany's ambitions, especially in air power, it can be argued that World War II might never have happened. As it was, Germany's appetite for expansion was only fueled.

Even at this stage it was far from certain that Germany would not rest on its territorial gains. Some European nations were still not convinced there would be a second twentieth-century war with Germany. On 6 December 1938 a Franco-German pact was agreed as a result of Munich which served to guarantee borders between the two nations. At this time spending on the air forces of several countries increased, including those of Britain, Belgium and France.

Far more relevant to the atmosphere of the period was an agreement of 31 March 1939 in which Britain and France guaranteed assistance to Greece, Poland and Romania in the event of invasion by Germany. Whether or not Germany took this seriously in the light of the events of 1938 cannot be stated, but on 22 August final orders were given for the pending German invasion of Poland. At the same time von Ribbentrop signed a non-aggression treaty with the Soviet Union which was scheduled to last 10 years, just as Poland's had in 1934, but also included mention of the partition of Poland. By the end of August it was only a question of time before Germany invaded Poland and general mobilisation was ordered in Britain. The invasion began on 1 September. On the following day Britain deployed 10 squadrons of Fairey Battle light bombers in France and on the 3rd, in accordance with the pact they had with Poland, Britain and France declared war on Germany after their ultimatum for German forces to withdraw from Poland had been ignored.

Below: *Dornier Do 17Z-2s undertook some of the earliest Luftwaffe operations during the Polish campaign.*

Above: *An example of the PZL P.11c has been preserved at Krakow in Poland.*

Germany had invaded Poland in the belief that the Polish Army Air Force operated some 900 warplanes. In fact the true number of combat-ready warplanes was nearer one-third of this total. Therefore Germany committed two of its four Luftflotten (Air Fleets); Luftflotte 1 under the command of Flight General Kesselring, Eastern Commander of the Luftwaffe, and Luftflotte 4 under Flight General Löhr, South-Eastern Commander. Luftflotte 2 was at this time under the command of Flight General Felmy. Northern Commander, and Luftflotte 3 under Flight General Sperrle, Western Commander. Luftflotten 1 and 4 had at their disposal about 900 bombers and dive bombers, including all nine Ju 87 Stukagruppen (which included those from Luftflotte 3), Heinkel He 111s, Dornier Do 17s and Henschel Hs 123s. These were complemented by a large number of fighters in the form of Messerschmitt Bf 109s and twin-engined escort Bf 110s, divided into offensive and defensive forces. In addition, vast numbers of Junkers Ju 52/3m transports, Henschel Hs 126 reconnaissance aircraft and other types were employed during the invasion.

Poland's fighting aircraft were both outnumbered and ill deployed, with an interceptor-fighter force made up of near-obsolete types. The most numerous Polish fighter was the PZL P.11, an open-cockpit single-seater using strut-braced Pulawski-type gull wings, a fixed undercarriage and armed with two or four guns. Many aircraft lacked a radio and all used Polish-built versions of British Bristol Mercury IV-S2, V-S2 and VI-S2 (of 500-645hp) or French Gnome-Rhône

9K Mistral (of 525-595hp) radial engines. Indeed, the use of foreign-designed engines was symptomatic of Poland's aircraft industry in the 1930s; given the good factories and very competent workforce it was underfunded and under-utilized, with an undue emphasis on exports necessitated by the indigenous air force's small budget.

At the time of the invasion of Poland, only 128 P.11s were fit for combat. Examples of the P.11c were capable of 390km/h (242mph) and these were supplemented by 30 older 317km/h (197mph) P.7as and perhaps a single more modern and much more powerful P.24a. This interceptor-fighter force was complemented by a handful of worthless LWS 4 Zubr twin-engined bomber monoplanes, about half of the 90 PZL P.37 Los twin-engined medium bombers delivered, more than 120 useful PZL P.23B and P.43A Karaś three-seat light bombers (of 215 delivered, a figure which included P.23A dual-control trainers and five P.43As intended for export), and a mish-mash of other aircraft including a large number of slow and antiquated Lublin XIII two-seat reconnaissance and army co-operation monoplanes.

By far the most competent Polish warplane was the P.37 Los, a totally modern high-performance mid-wing bomber that had first entered service with the Lotnictwo Wojskowe in 1938. Produced initially with a single fin-and-rudder tail unit but later featuring twin vertical surfaces, the Los carried a crew of four and could fly at up to 440km/h (273mph) on the power of its two license-built Bristol Pegasus engines (the P.37B Los B used Pegasus XXs of 925hp). Armed for defense with three 7.7mm machine guns in nose, dorsal and ventral positions, its offensive load was a respectable 2600kg (5730lb), perhaps made up of twenty 50kg or 110kg bombs or two of 1300kg.

Although the Karaś was the most important Polish bomber in terms of numbers immediately available for action on 1 September 1939, the Los was in fact the best. Actually intended for both reconnaissance and bombing duties, the Karaś had entered Polish service in 1936. A cantilever low-wing monoplane with a fixed undercarriage and powered by a 680hp Polish-built Pegasus VIII engine in the P.23B version, it could manage a speed of 319km/h (198mph). Armament comprised one fixed forward-firing machine gun and two more in rear-firing dorsal and ventral positions, plus up to 700kg (1540lbs) of bombs could be carried under the wing.

Just prior to the invasion, Polish aircraft had been deployed to their secret wartime airfields away from the peacetime bases well known to the Germans. Though small and flying many outdated aircraft, the Lotnictwo Wojskowe flung everything it had at the Germans from 1 September. The interceptor-fighter strength was split into two distinct forces, four squadrons of the 1st Air Regiment and a P.7a squadron forming the Pursuit Brigade to defend Warsaw and the remaining force unwisely divided into small, widely spread groups to work with the Polish army. Unfortunately the defenders lacked an adequate number of replacement aircraft held in reserve, spare component parts and an early warning system, all of which contributed to a degraded fighting capability.

The Pursuit Brigade initially proved particularly successful, stopping two German bombing raids on Warsaw on the first day and gaining air victories over a dozen Luftwaffe bombers. But in the process 10 of its own fighters had been destroyed and many more damaged. A kill-to-loss ratio close to one-to-one would not achieve deliverance.

Battles were taking place all over Poland, with the Luftwaffe heavily committed to destroying Polish airfields, communications, ground forces, factories and other strategic and non-strategic targets. Apart from the defense of Warsaw itself, the major activity of the Polish air force was to slow down and destroy German ground forces as they advanced. With the PZL fighters rising skyward to head off Luftwaffe warplanes, Karaś and Los bombers pressed home many sorties against German armor, achieving notable success but with neither the number of aircraft nor replacements to allow for the inevitable losses. Much of the fighting was concentrated around the area of Radomsko and Piotrkow, a vital route to Warsaw itself.

The ferocity of the Polish defense was well illustrated on 3 September, when Polish defenders both on the ground and in the air claimed four Dornier Do 17 and two Heinkel He 111 bombers, three Junkers Ju 87 and one Henschel Hs 123 dive bombers, two Messerschmitt Bf 109 and three Bf 110 fighters, one Junkers Ju 52 transport, two Fieseler Fi 156 and three Henschel Hs 126 liaison and reconnaissance aircraft, and one Heinkel He 59 multi-engined reconnaissance biplane. But this was the best day for the defenders and more and more Polish aircraft were lost as each kilometer was fought for.

Below: *The most numerous serviceable Polish warplane in September 1939 was the P.23 Karaś, surviving examples that fled across the border to Romania later serving with the Romanian air force on the Soviet Front.*

Above: *Aircrew prepare to board a Heinkel He 111. The dorsal gun position on some aircraft (as here) had a 'lobster'-type rear section through which the gun projected, allowing it to be fully enclosed before combat.*

Right: *The swinging crutch of a Ju 87 was designed to throw the bomb clear of the airscrew while dive-bombing.*

Opposite: *A Luftwaffe mechanic carries a bomb to a waiting Ju 87.*

Lacking fuel and all other essentials, the aircrews, fighters and bombers of the Lotnictwo Wojskowe fought on, knowing the consequence of allowing the Luftwaffe freedom of the air. By the 16th only about 50 Polish fighters plus surviving bombers continued the resistance, with the main concentration of strength in the east of the country. Then, on 17 September, Soviet forces poured into Poland and the fight was as good as over. With disastrously little fuel left, an attempt was made to save the remaining Polish aircraft in the hope of finding a new way to help the nation, and on that day a total of about 38 fighters, nearly 60 Karaś and Los bombers plus other aircraft fled abroad, mostly to Romania.

With air opposition gone, the Luftwaffe made the most of the opportunity to wreak havoc and within a short time the war was over, marked by the surrender of 17,000 Polish troops at Kock. The Luftwaffe had lost 285 aircraft during the Polish campaign with nearly as many seriously damaged. More than 400 German aircrew were dead or missing. The brave but outmatched and outnumbered Lotnictwo Wojskowe had lost the majority of its fighters, well over 100 Karaś but only 26 Los bombers, proving that had it modernized more quickly prior to the conflict it might have inflicted unacceptable losses upon the invaders. Indeed, among the new aircraft under development in 1939 was a high-speed twin-engined multi-purpose fighter to replace the P.11 and a similar type of attack aircraft with which to equip their Karaś squadrons.

From the German viewpoint, while the Polish campaign had seen victory, the near-obsolete fighters that opposed Luftwaffe aircraft had proved more effective in combat than expected. But the belief that the Lotnictwo Wojskowe had begun the war with many more aircraft than was the case and that many Luftwaffe sorties met only thin resistance led to wrong assumptions about the capabilities of Luftwaffe aircraft. The classic of all misconceptions centered upon the Junkers Ju 87 'Stuka'. This two-seat cranked-wing dive bomber, with its heavily faired fixed undercarriage and inadequate

machine gun protection, was cumbersome and could manage only 380km/h (236mph) on the power of a 1200hp Junkers Jumo 211Da engine in its Ju 87B form.

The Ju 87 had first entered service in 1937 and undertook a minor role in the air war in Spain. By late 1939, however, it was a somewhat outdated design, its two fixed forward-firing guns supplemented only by a single rear-firing machine gun for defense against enemy attack. One 500kg or 250kg bomb was normally carried under the fuselage and released by a swinging crutch that kept the bomb clear of the propeller during its near-vertical attacking dive, while smaller bombs could increase the warload.

During the Polish campaign the Ju 87B had achieved all its objectives, using the accuracy of dive bombing to attack selected strategic targets and softening enemy defenses. Some 300 had taken part in the campaign, but only 31 were lost in action. So the 'Stuka' myth was born, enhanced by the very ugliness of its appearance. Convinced of its continued worth in battle, Air Minister and Commander-in-Chief of the German air arm Field Marshal Hermann Göring ordered the Ju 87 to remain in production. Indeed, as no suitable replacement was forthcoming, it was still being built in 1944, by which time more than 5000 had left the lines. Although 1939 had created a legend, 1940 would witness the truth.

The other aircraft that participated in the Polish campaign had come out quite well, although certain inadequacies had been revealed. The most numerous medium bombers in Luftwaffe service in September 1939 were

Below: A Luftwaffe Messerschmitt Bf 109E-3 fighter, pictured in 1940.

the Dornier Do 17 and Heinkel He 111. The former had first entered Luftwaffe service in 1937 in bomber and reconnaissance models and a number of the original production Do 17Es and Fs were still on strength in September 1939. The most numerous version of the Do 17 bomber, however, was the Do 17Z, a five-seater powered by two 1000hp Bramo 323P Fafnir radial engines in Do 17Z-2 form and capable of a little over 400km/h (250mph). It was defended by six machine guns and, though its offensive warload was not high at only 1000kg (2200lbs), its range was more than reasonable.

Do 17s participated thereafter in the campaigns against France, Britain and the Soviet Union, but not Norway; 1942 saw its last major use as a bomber. The He 111, on the other hand, was prominent as a bomber and missile launch aircraft throughout World War II. The first prototype He 111 had appeared in 1935 — before even the Ju 87 — but it was then a transport with military potential. Early bomber versions of the He 111 came off production lines in 1936, and by February of the following year a considerable number were in Spain for operational evaluation with the Condor Legion.

These and subsequent early models of the He 111 used the traditional stepped-type forward fuselage, with the pilot looking out over a long, partially-glazed nose. However, a major redesign of the fuselage produced the He 111P with the asymmetrically-positioned fully-glazed bubble nose, through which the pilot and nose gunner had excellent forward and side views. This arrangement became standard thereafter. Delivery of the He 111P began in early 1939 and was followed by the He 111H, the main difference between the two marks being the later subtype's use of Junkers Jumo 211 engines instead of the Daimler-Benz DB 601s fitted to the He 111P.

By the time of the Polish invasion the Luftwaffe possessed about 800 He 111s. About 700 — almost entirely He 111Ps and Hs — were in a fit state for combat, but by no means all were for use in Poland. Early He 111Ps could attain a maximum speed of 400km/h (248mph) and carried a warload twice that of the Do 17. Surprisingly, little thought had been given during the configurational update of the bomber to increasing defensive armament (originally just three machine guns) or providing armor to protect the aircrew. While later production models went some way towards correcting these faults, the Luftwaffe lost nearly 80 He 111s during the Polish campaign. He 111s undertook attacks on naval and other targets and conducted mass raids on Warsaw and elsewhere.

The two Messerschmitt fighters, the single-seat and single-engined Bf 109 and the two/three-seat twin-engined long-range Bf 110, suffered mixed fortunes, although both types were among the best aircraft available to the Luftwaffe in September 1939 and were used throughout World War II. The Bf 109, first flown as a prototype in 1935 and

blooded in Spain during the Civil War, was the main fighter for the Polish campaign. One of the principal versions used against Poland was the then-latest Bf 109E, a 1050hp Daimler-Benz DB 601A-engined aircraft with two cannon and two machine guns. Indeed, the 'Emil' remained the Luftwaffe's standard version for the first two war years. Capable of 550km/h (342mph) in early form and highly maneuverable, with the pilot comfortable in the fully-enclosed cockpit, it far outperformed any Polish opposition and so was not too troubled by the PZL defenders which, overall, accounted for more than 120 confirmed victories against the Luftwaffe. Six Bf 109s were destroyed by the guns of Los bombers but the majority of the 60-plus Bf 109s lost during the Polish campaign were undoubtedly brought down by ground anti-aircraft fire. This resulted from the widespread use of the fighter to strafe Polish ground forces, the necessarily low altitude of such attacks greatly reducing speed and increasing vulnerability.

The twin-engined Messerschmitt Bf 110 undertook bomber escort and then ground attack roles during September 1939, its first major task being to escort bombers attacking

Above: *Messerschmitt Bf 109s operated by Lehrgeschwader 1 (instructional group 1).*

Right: *Mechanics work on the engine of a Bf 109 fighter-bomber of 8/JG 53.*

Polish cities and airfields. The Bf 110s initially suffered mixed fortune against Polish PZL fighters, although on balance the greater maneuverability of the single-seaters was overcome and Bf 110s inflicted more losses than they sustained during air combat. Unfortunately for the Luftwaffe, the number of Bf 110Cs available for the campaign was small, with all three Zerstörergruppen (heavy fighter groups) participating. Armed with two cannon and five machine guns, the DB 601A-1-engined Bf 110C-1 could attain 540km/h (336mph), a speed far greater than any Polish warplane. Very few Bf 110s were lost during the fighting in Poland, although defense forces claimed three on 3 September alone, the Luftwaffe's most disastrous single day for air losses.

All through the Polish campaign the German high command had been fearful of foreign intervention, gambling that the governments of France and Britain would not take massive retaliation for the invasion of Poland even though war had been declared. As previously mentioned, 10 RAF squadrons of Fairey Battle light bombers of the Advanced Air Striking Force, led by No 226 Squadron, had been deployed in France on 2 September 1939, followed days later by 13 squadrons of Bristol Blenheim high-performance bombers, Hawker Hurricane single-seat fighters and Westland Lysander army co-operation aircraft for the AASF and Air Component. Gloster Gladiator biplane fighters followed in November after French requests to build up the fighter strength, with aircraft from Nos 607 and 615 Squadrons leaving Britain.

Europe was in a peculiar state at this time, with Britain and France having declared war on Germany yet maintaining fairly low profiles in the hope that a political solution could still be found. Germany's actions, on the other hand, were tempered by the realization that it lacked the reserve forces, fuel and ammunition for a sustained conflict with British and French forces either during or immediately after the Polish campaign. Although Germany still had designs upon other countries, its greatest need was to make up for the losses incurred during the Polish campaign, regroup and strengthen. This would take time.

This situation in Europe came to be termed 'the Phoney War.' For, although war with Germany had begun — indeed, air-raid sirens had sounded in London within an hour of the declaration — very little actual conflict was taking place. Of course there was enemy activity over Britain and continental Europe but, as the Luftwaffe was ordered not to seek unnecessary combat, this was kept to single aircraft or small-formation incursions. The Phoney War was to last until April-May 1940.

The first RAF aircraft to fly over Germany after war had been declared was a Blenheim

Left: *Luftwaffe Bf 110 twin-engined fighters sweep low over the countryside.*

Right: *The Gloster Gladiator was the RAF's only operational biplane fighter to serve in World War II.*

Below: *The Blenheim I was followed into RAF service by the longer-range and better-armed Blenheim IV (pictured), featuring an extended glazed nose to improve the navigator's position.*

of No 139 Squadron, which had carried out a reconnaissance of German naval vessels leaving Wilhelmshaven on 3 September. That night Armstrong Whitworth Whitley III bombers of Nos 51 and 58 Squadrons dropped six million anti-war propaganda leaflets on Bremen, Hamburg and the Ruhr. The following day 10 Blenheim IVs undertook the first Bomber Command attack of the war, striking at the German fleet in Schillig Roads off Wilhelmshaven. On the 5th a coastal reconnaissance Avro Anson twin-engined monoplane – a 1936 military derivative of a small six-passenger commercial airliner – attacked a German U-boat.

But the RAF was not having it all its own way. On 4 September a force of 14 Vickers Wellington twin-engined bombers of Nos 9 and 149 Squadrons had followed the Blenheims in attacking German naval targets, aiming to destroy the warships *Scharnhorst* and *Gneisenau* off Brunsbüttel. During the course of this raid, a Bf 109E of II/JG 77 (Luftflotte 4) brought down a Wellington of No 9 Squadron. On 30 September Bf 109Es of JG 53 brought down all but one of five Battle light bombers of No 150 Squadron undertaking a reconnaissance mission. This revenged an RAF success of the 20th, when Sgt F. Letchford, the rear gunner of a No 88 Squadron Battle operating with the AASF in France, had destroyed a Messerschmitt Bf 109E, recording the first German aircraft to be shot down by the RAF since 1918.

The Fairey Battle had been designed as a modern monoplane replacement for the RAF's Hawker Hind biplane, and indeed its sleek cantilever low-wing configuration, with a retractable main undercarriage and enclosed accommodation for the three crew, certainly appeared a giant step forward. Its maximum speed and warload of 388km/h (241mph) and 454kg (1000lbs) respectively was a great improvement over the Hind's 299km/h (186mph) and 227kg (500lb) bombload. In consequence the Battle became a stalwart of the RAF's expansion program in the late 1930s. Like many other aircraft of the period, however, it had become near-obsolete by the outbreak of war but its massive service use guaranteed it a major role during 1939-40.

The Battle bomber carried a similar two-gun armament to the old Hind, with a single forward-firing gun and a rear-mounted gun fired from the end of the long fuselage canopy. Although Poland had wanted to import the Battle for its air force, its antiquated-looking Karaś probably performed bettter than the faster Battle by virtue of its greater all-round defensive capability. Ironically, however, the first Polish squadrons formed within RAF Bomber Command were equipped with Battles.

To Germany's annoyance, Spain had declared its neutrality to the European war on 3 September. It was no surprise when the United States followed suit two days later. Enemy activity in the skies over Britain during the early war months was little more than random attacks on naval bases, sea ports and shipping. Like the RAF, the Luftwaffe was not ready to upset the equilibrium with attacks on mainland soil.

Another favored activity at this time was reconnaissance, and it was during such a Luftwaffe mission that an important chain of events was triggered. On 26 September 1939

Above: Blackburn Skuas of No 803 Squadron, FAA, in flight off the coast of Britain.

the Royal Navy aircraft carrier HMS *Ark Royal* was sailing off Norway, escorted by the battlecruisers HMS *Hood* and *Renown*, the battleships HMS *Rodney* and *Nelson*, and various other vessels. Three Luftwaffe Dornier Do 18 twin-engined patrol and reconnaissance flying boats of Küstenfliegergruppe 106 (coastal group 106) spotted the British vessels and began to shadow them, reporting their position. On board HMS *Ark Royal* were Blackburn Skua two-seat naval fighter and dive bomber monoplanes of Nos 801 and 803 Squadrons. These were five-gun (four forward-firing and one rear-mounted),

890hp Bristol Perseus XII-powered aircraft that had entered FAA service shortly before the war, each possessing a maximum speed of just 362km/h (225mph). The Skuas were joined on the carrier by Fairey Swordfish torpedo-reconnaissance biplanes. Patrolling Swordfish spotted the Dorniers and nine Skuas were immediately launched from the carrier. The Skuas pressed home their attacks on the Dorniers, but only one was forced down. Once the crew had been saved, the stricken Do 18 was sunk. This was the very first FAA (Fleet Air Arm) victory of World War II.

Meanwhile, in response to the reconnaissance of the Do 18s, Junkers Ju 88A bombers of I/KG 30 had taken off to attack the British vessels, with a particular eye upon the carrier. During the course of the actual attack, HMS *Hood* was hit by a 500kg bomb but this bounced from it into the sea without exploding. Although one Luftwaffe pilot was sure he had hit *Ark Royal*, no damage was sustained.

The true significance of the Ju 88 attack was not its failure to sink the *Ark Royal* but that this represented the very first operational use of the bomber, I/KG 30 having been formed just four days earlier. The Ju 88A-1, the initial production version, was powered by two 1200hp Junkers Jumo 211 engines and possessed a maximum speed of 450km/h (279mph). Unlike earlier bombers used by the Luftwaffe, it had adequate defensive armament, comprising five/seven machine guns, while its warload carried internally and externally was up to 2000kg (4410lbs) of bombs.

The Ju 88 became one of the outstanding combat aircraft of World War II, the same basic airframe serving as a bomber, night fighter, reconnaissance aircraft, tank and

Below: A Junkers Ju 88A with bombs attached to its underwing racks prepares for take-off.

trainbuster/ground-attack aircraft, and finally the unmanned explosives-carrying lower component of the little-used Mistel composite 'missile.'

A Dornier Do 18 was again the victim in a wartime 'first' on 8 October 1939, when an RAF Lockheed Hudson from No 224 Squadron brought one down over Jutland. The significance is that this was the first German aircraft to fall victim to a United States-built aircraft. The Hudson was a five-seat coastal patrol derivative of the Lockheed 14 Super Electra airliner, ordered as an emergency measure by the British Purchasing Commis-

sion in the US in 1938. Armed with two nose guns, usually a power-operated dorsal turret with two further guns, and a ventral gun plus 340kg (750lbs) of bombs, the Mk I could attain 396km/h (246mph) on the power of two 1100hp Wright Cyclone radial engines. Hundreds of Hudsons were employed by Coastal Command for their original purpose up to 1944, with one becoming the first RAF aircraft to attack and sink a German U-boat using rockets (May 1943 while based in North Africa). Meanwhile, the capabilities of the Hudson were enhanced by the introduction of ASV radar in 1940.

Similar aircraft were also used by the USAAF and US Navy as A-28/A-29s and PBOs respectively. The larger and more powerful Lockheed 18 transport also formed the basis of a bombing aircraft at British instigation, resulting in the well-defended Ventura for the RAF, USAAF and US Navy and the more specialized Lockheed PV-2 Harpoon for the latter service.

The attack upon HMS *Ark Royal* in September 1939 was only one incident that marked the Luftwaffe's early campaign against shipping and naval targets, the Junkers Ju 88 and Heinkel He 111 being prominent participants. During October German aircraft ventured over the UK to attack the Firth of Forth and Scapa Flow anchorages. The first major incident came on 16 October, when nine Ju 88As penetrated the Firth of Forth. Two British warships sustained some damage from the attack, but two Ju 88As were brought down in the sea by RAF Supermarine Spitfires of Nos 602 and 603 Squadrons, becoming the first German aircraft shot down over Britain during this war. The following day four Ju 88As raided Scapa Flow, causing damage to a battleship. Meanwhile, Heinkel He 111s had engaged

Below: A Lockheed A-29, the USAAF equivalent of the RAF Hudson.

the same target areas; on 26 October an He 111P was forced to land on Scottish soil some five miles south of the Firth of Forth, the first German aircraft to do so.

Attacks on naval targets continued throughout the winter of 1939-40, a situation made worse by the Luftwaffe dropping magnetic anti-shipping mines in British coastal waters from mid November. Elsewhere, on 30 November the Soviet air force carried out the opening attacks of the so-called 'Winter War' with Finland. While the

Luftwaffe and the RAF played out a kind of deadly chase game over Britain, similar actions on the Western and other fronts were taking place. Over France both the Armée de l'Air and the RAF's AASF were in action against German intruders, with Hurricanes scoring some notable victories. But when the Luftwaffe came into contact with France's latest fighter, the single-seat Morane-Saulnier MS 406, it soon became patently clear that the French fighter was little match for the Bf 109, although it was perhaps more

maneuverable than its adversary.

The MS 406, which had joined the Armée de l'Air in 1939 and was in substantial production, possessed the external characteristics of a modern fighter – a low cantilever wing, retractable undercarriage and an enclosed cockpit for the pilot. However, its Hispano 12Y-31 engine produced only 850hp, giving the fighter a top speed of just 490km/h (304mph). The Bloch 151, another new French fighter with a 920hp Gnome-Rhône 14N 35 engine, was even slower,

while the similar but higher-powered Bloch 152 could attain 520km/h (323mph) on its 1080hp Gnome-Rhône engine. Unfortunately the Bloch 152 was only gradually becoming combat capable in 1939-40, as only after France declared war on Germany were any of the 151/152s already delivered provided with propellers or gunsights. The aircraft the Armée de l'Air needed most desperately was the Dewoitine D 520, a fighter far superior to the Morane-Saulnier and Bloch types and capable of 550km/h(342mph) on

Above: *The versatile Lockheed Ventura served the US and British forces in the bombing, anti-submarine and training roles.*

the power of an engine similar to that in the MS 406. However, D 520s only began to enter operational service in February 1940.

By March 1940, it was clear that the honeymoon period of the war was drawing to a close. The Luftwaffe had been accepting large numbers of new aircraft and German manufacturing production was set at a level that could sustain substantial losses from combat and attrition. The increasing frequency with which Allied aircraft met the previously scarce Bf 110 was proof of this. Indeed, the Bf 110 had been responsible in part for the British decision not to continue daylight formation bomber raids after 18 December 1939, following the RAF's loss of half a force of 24 Vickers Wellingtons on a reconnaissance mission to Wilhelmshaven, the Jade Estuary and Schillig Roads on that date. Of the 12 Wellingtons lost during the great air battle that erupted after interception by Bf 109s and Bf 110s, nine fell to the guns of Bf 110s. German losses were two Bf 109s to RAF air gunners.

March 1940 was significant in other respects. By the 12th Finland's fight against the overwhelming Soviet forces was at an end and the nation capitulated. Its air force at the

time of the initial Soviet invasion in late November 1939 was hardly modern by any standards, but neither was the Soviet air force. Finland used three types of fighter plane in small numbers: the 285km/h (177mph) Bristol Bulldog open-cockpit biplane carrying two machine guns, the Gloster Gladiator, and 45 Dutch-designed but mostly locally-built Fokker D XXIs. The latter served with the 2nd Air Regiment.

While the Bulldog really belonged to an earlier era – the RAF having operated it between 1929 and 1937 – the D XXI's only failing was its use of a fixed and faired under-carriage instead of the now common retract-able type. Armed with four guns and capable of 460km/h (286mph) on the power of its 830hp Bristol Mercury radial engine, it was not up to the latest Western standards but was well suited to the fight against Soviet aircraft although scarce in number. A D XXI of HLeLv24, flown by Sergeant Kukkonen,

took the decision not to restrict the activities of RAF Bomber Command to offshore German targets; on the night of 19-20 March a force of 30 Armstrong Whitworth Whitley and 20 Handley Page Hampden twin-engined bombers raided the German sea-plane base on the island of Sylt at Hornum. This represented the RAF's first attack against a German land target, and the bombs from a Whitley of No 102 Squadron were therefore the first of the war to fall on German soil.

On 9 April 1940 Germany put Operation *Weserübung*, the invasion and occupation of Denmark and Norway, into effect. Like Finland, Denmark flew both Bulldog and D XXI fighters plus a number of locally-built 370km/h (230mph) British-designed Gloster Gauntlet biplanes. Not being in a position to put up a significant defense, Denmark was overrun virtually without bloodshed. Not so Norway, however.

Above: *The Dewoitine D 520 was the only French single-engined fighter able to compete on equal terms with the Messerschmitt Bf 109.*

became the first Finnish air loss of the Winter War when it was brought down by Finnish guns over Viipuri in an accident of identi-fication on 1 December 1939. On the same day Finland gained its first air victory when a D XXI of the same squadron, flown by Lt Eino Luukkanen, destroyed a Soviet Tupolev SB-2 bomber. Production of the D XXI in Finland with the US Pratt & Whitney Twin Wasp Junior engine of similar power to the Mercury began again in 1941, and these went into action during the later wartime campaigns which began in early 1941. Interestingly, in 1944 Finland produced its own fighter as the four-gun 530km/h (329mph) IvL Myrsky. Powered by Pratt & Whitney Twin Wasps, the 47 machines built were used to support Soviet forces fighting Germans from Finnish soil.

In March 1940 the British War Cabinet

At the start of the invasion of Norway, German forces landed on the coast and by air at Oslo and Stavanger, and British forces quickly became involved. The RAF was also occupied temporarily in its first anti-shipping mine operation of the war around the Danish coast. On 23 April the British aircraft carriers HMS *Ark Royal* and *Glorious* were sent there to support the combined forces of Norway, Britain and France, stationing off Andalsnes and Namsos. On board *Glorious* were examples of the Fleet Air Arm's final biplane fighter, the Gloster Sea Gladiator. Four-gunned fighters with enclosed cockpits and capable of 394km/h (245mph) from their Mercury engines, Sea Gladiators of No 804 Squadron were used to protect the 18 RAF Gladiators of No 263 Squadron being ferried to Norway by *Glorious*. The Gladiators were flown to

Above: *A Finnish-built, Mercury-engined Fokker D XXI, delivered to the 2nd Air Regiment. Finnish D XXIs were often employed to strafe Soviet transports and ski troops, flying low to avoid enemy fighters.*

Left: *A camouflaged Finnish Gloster Gladiator biplane fighter. The swastika symbol was used well before the emergence of the German Nazi Party.*

frozen Lake Lesjaskog, from where they were to operate.

Interestingly, the most important German fighter of the Norway campaign was again the Bf 110, which dealt a swift blow to the dozen Norwegian Gladiators and destroyed the majority of RAF Gladiators on the ground before they had a chance to make any impact. The fighting for Norway continued for some while, but did not put off the greatest German campaign up to this point – the invasion of the Low Countries. Eventu-ally, HMS *Glorious* left Norwegian waters with what remained of two Gladiator squadrons on board, but was attacked and sunk on 8 June by the German battleships *Gneisenau* and *Scharnhorst*, the two warships RAF Wellingtons had attempted to bomb out of existence back in September 1939. By early May 1940 German forces appeared invincible, and yet they still had to face the combined power of Belgium, France, Holland and Great Britain, with Norway still hanging on.

CHAPTER 2

THE LUFTWAFFE SPREAD

With its eastern flank secured by the occupation of Poland and the treaty with the Soviet Union, and the northern flank all but secure with the occupation of Denmark and Norway's near collapse, Germany's attention turned westward.

On 10 May 1940 Germany began its invasion of the Low Countries with Belgium and the Netherlands. This saw the first major use of paratroops, aeroplane- and glider-borne assault troops and Blitzkrieg tactics (simultaneous lightning attack by air and ground armor). Opposed by the combined air forces of Belgium, France and Holland, together with a substantial RAF presence and Norway still heroically fighting on, the Luftwaffe met determined resistance. Though superior in quantity and quality of fighters and bombers, the Luftwaffe suffered its worst losses, that first day seeing 304 aircraft destroyed and 740 aircrew killed, missing or wounded.

Most vulnerable were Junkers Ju 52/3m transports carrying paratroops and airborne troops and supplies – of an available 430 Ju 52s, 157 were lost that day, while many more crashed but were later repaired. Of the 157 lost, 39 were brought down by Dutch D XXIs in a single action. He 111 bombers were the worst hit of the offensive forces, with 51 destroyed on the one day, although this should be viewed in the light that about half of the total bomber forces of more than 1100 aircraft available to the Luftwaffe for this campaign were He 111s. In addition, 26 Dornier Do 17s and 18 Ju 88s were destroyed, but only nine Ju 87s. Fighter losses were small, with only six Bf 109s lost of a force exceeding 1000 with Luftflotte 2 and Luftflotte 3, and a single Bf 110 out of a strength of nearly 250.

While the Luftwaffe continued to take substantial losses, the mish-mash of Allied aircraft thrown into battle were no match. France's 500 or so single-seat fighters were mainly MS 406s, accompanied by Blochs, a very small number of D 520s and US-built fighters in the form of Curtiss Hawk 75s. The latter were export P-36 Mohawks, each possessing a speed of 483km/h (300mph) from a 1050hp Pratt & Whitney R-1830 Twin Wasp radial engine. Despite being incredibly lightly armed, Hawk 75s were responsible for the destruction of two Bf 109s on the first occasion the opposing fighters met.

Right: *Messerschmitt's Bf 110 was not sufficiently maneuverable to escape RAF single-seaters.*

Left: *No fewer than 157 Junkers Ju 52/3ms, similar to the example pictured, were lost by the Luftwaffe on 10 May 1940.*

Right: *A Fokker GIA in wartime markings. The type was used to great effect by the Dutch against the attacking German forces.*

Above: *The LeO 451 was the finest French bomber of 1940.*

These were supplemented by 230 serviceable twin-engined 445km/h (277mph) Potez 630/631s (each carrying seven machine guns and a cannon). To the French fighter force could be added the RAF's 60 or so Hurricanes and Gladiators, the small number of Belgian Hurricanes and Gladiators, and Dutch D XXIs and Fokker GI twin-engined, twin-boom ground-attack fighters capable of 475km/h (295mph) on two Bristol Mercury engines.

Allied bomber forces in continental Europe at this time were no better prepared for the German invasion, with Belgian and British strengths concentrated mainly on the outdated and slow three-seat Fairey Battle. Dutch hopes rested on the Fokker TV, a workmanlike five-seater capable of an impressive 417km/h (259mph) on two 925hp Bristol Pegasus XXVI radial engines, defended by six machine guns and able to carry a 1000kg (2205lb) bombload. Unfortunately the Dutch had received only 16 from 1938, of which just nine examples were combat capable.

France possessed a substantial bomber force in May 1940 but the equipment ranged from the excellent to the obsolete. The nationalization of most French aircraft, armament and engine manufacturers engaged in the production of military equipment in August 1936 had been intended to step up production and co-ordinate re-

armament. Instead, production of modern aircraft fell sharply. The Armée de l'Air had been expected to deploy several new bombers during the late 1930s – including the Amiot 350, Bloch 131, Bloch 175, Breguet 690, Lioré et Olivier 451 and Loire-Nieuport 41. All except for the Loire-Nieuport were twin-engined, the LN 41 being a single-seat cranked-wing dive bomber with a retractable undercarriage. However, the LN 41 had a disastrously low speed of only 260km/h (161mph), and the largest bomb it could carry was one of 225kg. Rejected by the Armée de l'Air, a small number went to the French Navy. Despite all its shortcomings, an aircraft of this type was missed by the Armée de l'Air when the German land armies poured into France in 1940.

Of the other bombers, the Amiot 350-series aircraft, capable of 485km/h (301mph) and with a bombload of between 800 and 1200kg, were delivered during 1940 but were unable to be used. The 350km/h (218mph) Bloch 131 had arrived in service by 1939 but was considered unsuited to its intended role and was used by reconnaissance squadrons instead. The Bloch 175, a fine and fast light bomber capable of 520km/h (323mph) on two 1180hp Gnome-Rhône 14N radial engines and armed with five guns for defense and a warload of 1550kg (3417lbs), was exactly the caliber of aircraft the Armée de l'Air required but only 20 or so had left the factory by the fall of

France and none saw combat. Interestingly many near-complete aircraft were finished under German occupation and sent for testing by the victors.

The Breguet 690 light bomber, originally intended to be a high-performance twin-engined multi-role fighter, was produced in two main versions for the Armée de l'Air, as the 510km/h (317mph) Br 693 and 560km/h (348mph) Br 695. Only about half the Br 690 series aircraft built were taken into service, totalling about 140. By far the most numerous version was the 680hp Gnome-Rhône 14M-engined Br 693.

Without doubt the finest French bomber of the period was the four-seat Lioré et Olivier 451. Although modern in every sense, it was underpowered, with too little consideration of defensive armament and with unreliable

Below: *Partners in conflict. A French Armée de l'Air Amiot 143 (foreground) waits in readiness alongside an RAF Fairey Battle.*

systems, yet was nevertheless capable of 500km/h (311mph) on the power of two 1000hp Gnome-Rhône 14N20/21 engines and carried a 1400kg (3086lb) warload. Only 40 percent of the 450 LeO 451s built by the fall of France became operational, while later examples served with the Vichy government and the French Navy in Syria. The Luftwaffe also converted a number into transports.

In marked contrast to these modern bombers, the re-equipment programme had become so bogged down by slow production, faulty equipment or lack of component parts that many antique bombers had to be pressed into action against invading German forces. One of the best remembered of these was the Amiot 143, a twin-engined (870hp Gnome-Rhône 14K) day and night all-metal aircraft carrying just four machine guns for defense

and with internal stowage in the deep forward fuselage for 900kg (1984lbs) of bombs. Dating from 1933 and first joining the Armée de l'Air in 1935, it was a curious mixture of old and new, with its thick shoulder-mounted monoplane wing and very bulky fuselage supporting heavily-faired fixed undercarriage units. Maximum speed was just 305km/h (190mph). A contemporary of the Amiot was the Bloch 210, its two similar engines allowing a top speed of only 300km/h (186mph) despite the use of a low cantilever wing and a retractable undercarriage. In May 1940 approximately half the 300 Bloch 210s built were still in service.

France's only four-engined bombers available in May 1940 were equally outdated Farman F220-series aircraft that had joined the Armée de l'Air from 1936. Variously powered with Gnome-Rhône or Hispano-Suiza engines of 800 to 1100hp, they were high-wing monoplanes with fixed undercarriages. For defense against fighter attack

three machine guns were placed in manually-operated nose and dorsal turrets and a retractable ventral position, hardly adequate even by 1936 standards and totally useless in 1940. The offensive load, however, was fairly substantial at 4200kg (9259lbs). Maximum speed was 325km/h (202mph).

France even threw biplane bombers into the mêlée in May 1940. French Navy Lioré et Olivier H-257*bis* and less powerful LeO 258s operated as coastal bombing/torpedo floatplanes, while the former type in landplane form was flown by the Armée de l'Air as a bomber-reconnaissance aircraft. The H-257*bis* was powered by two 870hp Gnome-Rhône 14Kfrs radial engines, which bestowed a maximum speed of 250km/h (155mph). Armed with four machine guns, the offensive load was just 600kg (1323lbs) of bombs or a 670kg torpedo.

In addition to the fighters and bombers of French origin and the Hawk 75 from the US, France had ordered other warplanes from the US in an attempt to build up its forces as the situation in Europe deteriorated. Of course, France had not been alone in its attempt to purchase US aircraft, Britain and Norway among others having followed the same route. France ordered Curtiss P-40 Warhawks in the form of Hawk 81A-1

fighters but these were eventually diverted to the RAF as Tomahawk Is. A similar fate overtook Grumman F4F Wildcat fighters, ordered as G-36As but taken into British service. France was more successful with US bombers, actually receiving some Douglas DB-7s and Martin Marylands (Model 167Fs), plus Vought V-156s for the French Navy. Curtiss SBC-4 Helldiver dive-bomber biplanes were also too late to help France, however, a small number being diverted to serve with the RAF as Cleveland trainers.

Despite their age and obsolescence, the Armée de l'Air possessed no fewer than 91 Amiot 143s on 10 May 1940, of which all but 35 were with active units. Their first mission was to drop propaganda leaflets over Germany, after which they became more belligerent. Amiot 143s are best remembered for the action on 14 May, when 13 aircraft from Groupements 9 and 10 undertook a near-suicidal mission to destroy the bridges over the River Meuse at Sedan and thereby slow the advancing German armor. Farman bombers had also dropped leaflets over Germany before widespread fighting broke out in the Low Countries, thereafter operating at night. On the night of 7-8 June 1940, one of three civil examples of the Farman, requisitioned by the French Navy at the time

Above: *A Handley Page Hampden I medium bomber of the RAF. Hampdens and Whitleys were the first aircraft of that service to drop bombs on Germany during World War II.*

of France's declaration of war in 1939, became the very first Allied aircraft to bomb Berlin. This aircraft, the F2234 *Jules Verne*, had been converted to carry a 2000kg (4409lb) warload. Its mission using a circuitous route took 13½ hours.

Also called in for the attack on the bridges over the Meuse were the French Navy's Vought 156F and LN 41 dive bombers; like the Amiots, these sustained heavy losses. The Breguet 693s performed some useful early work against German positions in Belgium, each using its four machine guns, cannon and eight 50kg bombs in a ground-attack role.

RAF participation in the battle for the Low Countries, and especially the fight for France, was waged from both sides of the Channel. On 10 May Fairey Battles of No 12 Squadron attacked the Maastricht bridges in Belgium, some crews bravely sacrificing their lives in the attempt. The crew of one Battle, Flying Officer D.E. Garland and Sergeant T. Gray, were posthumously awarded Britain's highest military decoration, the Victoria Cross, for their part. A few days later a massive force of 71 RAF Battles from No 12 Squadron and four other units struck at Sedan, the focal point of much Allied action, but 40 aircraft were lost.

Meanwhile, Air Marshal Dowding of RAF Fighter Command had allowed a further four Hurricane squadrons to fly to France, making 10 in all by 12 May, although he was not happy with the prospect of weakening Britain's own (and later vital) Home Defense fighter force. At a very early stage in the

fighting it became clear that, however heroic the defence by the Allied aircraft on the continent, they were no match for the well-organized Luftwaffe which was capable of striking in force and depth.

On the night of 11-12 May a small force of Whitley bombers from Nos 77 and 102 Squadrons, together with Handley Page Hampdens, bombed German lines of communication leading to Holland centered on the railway complex close to München Gladbach. These were the first RAF bombs to fall on the German mainland. On the 15-16th, Whitleys, Wellingtons and Hampdens opened the RAF campaign of heavy strategic

Top: *A Heinkel He 111 of KG 26, Luftflotte 2, a Kampfgeschwader that flew the type operationally from the beginning of World War II.*

Above: *Fully armed Ju 88s stand ready as their aircrews receive final instructions before a mission.*

night raids on Germany, attacking the industrial Ruhr. Göring's personal insistence that the Reich would not be overflown by Allied aircraft had left important centers of industry and communications without adequate defensive protection, relying solely on flak from ground guns. The aircraft equal to the task was the Messerschmitt Bf 110 but, while fighting in the west continued, none could be spared. Once France had fallen, however, Nachtjagdgeschwader 1 was formed as the first component of a night-fighter force under Oberst Josef Kammhuber. This came into being on 20 July 1940, with initial deployment being at Venlo in the Netherlands. By September the Junkers Ju 88C-2 night fighter was in use.

On 14 May, during surrender negotiations at the Hague, Germany had threatened to destroy all Dutch cities from the air and, indeed, Rotterdam was attacked during the negotiations when a number of Luftwaffe aircraft failed to receive the 'abort mission' instructions. Over the following days Allied squadrons gradually retreated under the weight of the German advance. By 26 May the RAF had even brought the totally obsolete Hawker Hector open-cockpit biplane into the battle, using it to dive-bomb German infantry near Calais.

Throughout the invasion, the Heinkel He 111 had been the Luftwaffe's mainstay bomber. On 28 May the evacuation of British troops from Dunkirk began, with fighters from England attempting to patrol the beaches and protect the massed forces against Luftwaffe harassment. The Royal Navy warships and other craft involved in the evacuation provided prime targets for the Luftwaffe, with Ju 88s also participating in the mêlée on 29 May. By 4 June the Dunkirk evacuation had been completed, with 338,000 soldiers ferried to Britain to regroup for coming battles. About one-third of this huge army comprised French and Belgians.

The Battle for France began on 5 June, and just nine days later German forces entered Paris. From the 17th the final airworthy aircraft of the RAF's Advanced Air Striking Force were flown from Nantes to Tangmere in Sussex. Using the railway carriage in the Compiègne Forest – where Germany had suffered the humiliation of the 1918 surrender – as the setting, Hitler accepted France's 1940 capitulation and four days later hostilities ended.

Britain's Prime Minister prior to the invasion of the Low Countries had been Neville Chamberlain, who had promised 'peace in our time' in September 1938 after appeasing Germany with the promise of non-interference in the German occupation of the Czech Sudetenland. After 10 May 1940, however, Britain was ruled by a new coalition

Below: *The final series of Bf 110 night fighter built, the Bf 110G-4d/R3, carried the latest Lichtenstein SN-2 radar. This example was captured by the Allies in Holland.*

Above: *A Bristol Beaufighter in all-black night finish. This particular aircraft was built as a TF Mk.X anti-shipping strike fighter.*

government with Winston Churchill as Prime Minister.

Churchill had recognized the road along which Germany was heading very early in the 1930s, and in October 1933 had warned Parliament that Germany was fast becoming the most heavily-armed country in the world. Despite these early warnings, the RAF had not been allowed to expand in keeping with the newly-created Luftwaffe, as hopes were raised that some form of European disarmament was a possibility. By 1935, however, proposals to expand the RAF were not rejected by Parliament, helped undoubtedly by the German announcement of further rearmament. Equally importantly for the future, 1935 also witnessed the first steps taken by Britain's Air Defense Research Committee to develop radio direction finding, better known thereafter as radar. As Britain stood alone in July 1940, radar became vital to the continued free existence of the nation.

The first British experimental radar was built under the direction of Robert Watson Watt and this demonstrated its ability to detect aircraft as early as mid 1936. This first device proved to be twice as effective as the sound locator previously used, sending out pulses of radio energy which were then echoed back to a receiver from any aircraft within the beam. The world's first interception using radar occurred in November 1936, when RAF Gauntlet biplane fighters were directed to an airliner in flight.

Further research greatly improved the scope of radar detection until it became practicable to set up a series of 20 extremely large radar stations capable of detecting aircraft flying towards or away from Britain up to a range of 177km (110 miles) and altitude of 4575m (15,000ft). Known as Chain Home, the system was set up to scan along the south and east approaches to Britain, clearly the directions from which any oncoming hostile force would come. As later events proved, the Chain Home radar system was a major factor in the successful defense of the island during the Battle of Britain, allowing inferior numbers of interceptors the time to press home attacks on superior hostile forces without the need to mount exhausting and often fruitless patrols.

Germany, too, had been researching radar but had not achieved anything like Britain's progress by the outbreak of war. As Allied bomber raids on occupied Europe and Germany itself increased, so the urgency for proper radar defenses became acute and Germany built its own chain of radar stations. In many respects, however, Germany put even greater emphasis on the development of *Lichtenstein*, a lightweight airborne radar that could be used on Bf 110 and Ju 88 night fighters, these aircraft being distinguishable by their nose antenna. As the war progressed so radars became smaller and the types of radar-equipped aircraft increased.

Britain had also developed a light airborne radar, known as AI (Airborne Interception), and in fact used it some time before the Luftwaffe. The very first radar-equipped night fighters were Bristol Blenheim IFs, converted bombers each armed with five forward-firing machine guns and one in a dorsal turret, and carrying AI. The British radar did not use the elaborate antenna of the German aircraft. The first true night combat interception was made in July 1940 when Flying Officer Ashfield's Blenheim located a Luftwaffe bomber.

While the Blenheim IF led the way, its performance was not good enough to make full use of the radar. Waiting in the wings, however, was the Bristol Beaufighter, which joined the RAF during the autumn of 1940. Powered by two 1590hp Bristol Hercules XI radial engines, which bestowed a top speed for the two-seat Beaufighter IF of 520km/h (323mph), its first victim was a Junkers Ju 88 on 19 November 1940. Beaufighters caused great losses to the Luftwaffe during the night Blitz and the type proved a major factor in bringing it to an end in October. The Beaufighter went on to serve in later versions as a night and day fighter and anti-shipping strike aircraft, deployed also (like many other RAF aircraft) in the Western Desert, Middle East and in the Far East, where it caused such havoc to the Japanese that it became known as 'Whispering Death.'

Radar was also used later for navigation, blind bombing and the detection of naval targets. Coastal Command of the RAF made good use of ASV (Air to Surface Vessel) radar in the hunt for surfaced submarines. The uses and applications of radar grew steadily as the technology developed and eventually even wartime German jet fighters sprouted radar antenna.

After the fall of France in June 1940, Göring wasted little time regrouping for the onslaught on Great Britain. With nearly

Below: The excellent but incredibly slow 'Stringbag', alias the Fairey Swordfish, carried an 18-inch torpedo.

3000 warplanes at his disposal, based along a front stretching from Norway to the west of France, his mission was to draw out the RAF and destroy it in preparation for Operation *Sea Lion*, the invasion of Britain.

Although the campaign of the Advanced Air Striking Force on the continent had been a disaster, by July 1940 the RAF's home defense force was well organized though a little small. Operational airfields were well dispersed, with squadrons able to use their flying hours to best advantage thanks to the Chain Home radar and an excellent associated system of command control. Pilots flew on a rotation basis when possible, keeping morale high and battleweariness low, in marked contrast to the Luftwaffe. Aircraft production was also in good order.

Notwithstanding its massive strength, the Luftwaffe was in high spirits after the French campaign, which had witnessed the humiliation of the RAF as well as the British Army and French forces. There appeared little reason to think the destruction of the RAF's home-based forces would be any more difficult than its fight against the combined Allied air forces in Europe during May. The Heinkel He 111, which had been the main bomber during the May campaigns, was

Left: Close-up of the nose section of a Junkers Ju 88. A crew of four was usually carried.

gradually being superseded by the far superior Ju 88; the same was true of the Dornier Do 17, although both it and the He 111 were still serving in substantial numbers. The Luftwaffe also considered the Ju 87 of great importance, while the performance of its Bf 109 and Bf 110 fighters was legendary.

July 1940 saw only a gradual build-up of attacks and counterattacks, with the Fleet Air Arm making some important early raids on the French fleet anchored at Oran in an attempt to prevent the vessels falling into German Navy hands. Used on these attacks was the Fairey Swordfish, the FAA's antiquated-looking torpedo-bomber and reconnaissance biplane affectionately known as 'Stringbag'. A three-seater with open cockpits, capable of only 224km/h (139mph) on the power of a 690hp Bristol Pegasus IIIM radial engine, it had already performed excellent work during the defense of Norway and, despite the development of more modern replacement aircraft, was to see out the whole of World War II as a carrier-based aircraft operating in many theaters of war.

Early German raids from 10 July were confined mainly to naval targets, both on land and at sea. Convoys in the Channel were repeatedly attacked by Do 17s and Ju 87s. At this time Dover, Portsmouth and Portland were prime targets, although Luftwaffe aircraft met with determined resistance; a force of 15 Do 17Zs was scattered by RAF Hurricanes on 15 July. Meanwhile, on 14 July RAF aerial reconnaissance provided evidence of the Germans massing barges and equipment for Operation *Sea Lion*. Yet, despite this, the constant Luftwaffe attacks on shipping in the Channel forced the Admiralty to withdraw warships to safer waters. Convoys thereafter found the Straits of Dover particularly hazardous.

As July turned to August, the ferocity of Luftwaffe attacks and the scope of its targets grew rapidly. British fighters exploited the many hitherto unrecognized weaknesses in Luftwaffe bombers, but at cost to their own depleting force. Then, on 8 August 1940, the Battle of Britain began in earnest. After 12 August RAF stations, industrial and other land targets became more important than shipping to the Luftwaffe.

The Luftwaffe had been evolved mainly as a tactical air force – hard-hitting, fast-moving and ideally suited to Blitzkrieg operations. Its bomber force comprised nothing heavier than a twin-engined medium bomber and, indeed, four-engined heavy bombers were denied it throughout the war (with one or two fairly insignificant exceptions from 1943 onwards). For the defeat of Britain, the Luftwaffe had to take on a strategic role, crossing long stretches of water to bomb important military and industrial targets in an attempt to destroy fighting and production capacities. Then cities came under fire, to break the will of the people to continue the struggle. Luftwaffe fighters were also not entirely suited to this type of warfare, their earlier

free-ranging sweeps attaining far greater success than was achieved in the role of bomber escort. The Bf 109, though in many respects a superior fighter to the early marks of Spitfire and Hurricane, lacked range for this type of mission, while the Bf 110, despite its longer range and endurance, was not sufficiently maneuverable to escape the guns of RAF single-seaters.

In terms of numbers, the most important fighter available to the RAF at the beginning of the Battle of Britain was the Hawker

Above: *An RAF Hurricane I (foreground) flies in formation with a pair of Supermarine Spitfire IIAs.*

Hurricane, an eight-gun monoplane with fabric covering most of its metal tubular structure. Hurricane Is were capable of 509km/h (316mph) on the power of the vaunted 1030hp Rolls-Royce Merlin II or III inline engine. Having first entered service with the RAF in late 1937, the type equipped 30 squadrons at the start of the Battle of Britain. Later in 1940 more powerful versions of the Hurricane appeared in service, followed in turn by even more powerful and heavier-armed models used as fighter-

bombers. 'Hurribombers' served in many theaters, from Malta to Burma and the Western Desert, where the Hurricane IID's two 40mm guns 'busted' many of Rommel's battle tanks.

Less numerous in the Battle of Britain but ultimately to become the best-remembered fighter of all time was the RAF's Supermarine Spitfire, a later fighter than the Hurricane that joined the RAF in 1938. Of all-metal construction and initially armed with four and then eight guns, the Mk I

versions proved capable of 571km/h (355mph) while using the same engine as the early Hurricanes. Its elliptical wing gave it a shape that was recognisable even to civilians on the ground and its blistering performance ensured it became a legend in its time.

On 8 August 19 squadrons of Spitfires were active with the RAF. Over the ensuing years a great many versions of the Spitfire were produced as the Bf 109, Fw 190 and other German fighters first gained, then lost, the performance edge. Some Spitfires were intended for unarmed photographic reconnaissance missions and others were built as fighter-bombers, but the majority were pure fighters. The most powerful Merlin-engined Spitfire was the Mk XI; when fitted with a 1760hp Merlin 63 or 63A engine it managed 679km/h (422mph). From 1943 Rolls-Royce Griffon-powered variants came on to the scene, most capable of both fighter and fighter-bomber duties. Many of these had engines of 2050hp or more. The widely-operated Spitfire XIV had a top speed of 721km/h (448mph). Though not the fastest version by any means, the Mark XIV had several claims to fame, not least for the destruction of the first Messerschmitt Me 262 jet fighter by the RAF, in October 1944, and for achieving an excellent record as a destroyer of V1 unmanned flying-bombs (launched against Britain from French sites from 13 June 1944). Well over 20,000 Spitfires of all versions were built before, during and after the war. This figure excludes the Seafire naval versions which entered FAA service from mid 1942 following the successful use of Sea Hurricanes on carriers and the expendable Hurricane 'Catafighters' launched by catapult from Merchant vessels in an attempt to protect convoys from German and Italian maritime aircraft (like the Luftwaffe's four-engined Focke-Wulf Fw 200 Condor).

Alongside Hurricanes and Spitfires at the start of the Battle of Britain were Boulton Paul Defiants, a small number of outdated Gloster Gladiator biplanes, and Bristol Blenheim IF night fighters possessing a speed of 418km/h (260mph) on the power of two 840hp Bristol Mercury VIII radial engines. US-built Brewster Buffalos, ordered by the British Purchasing Mission in 1939 and delivered in 1940 (together with those originally destined for conquered Belgium), became available for use from September but were adjudged unfit for the Western Front and served later in the Far East fighting the Japanese. The other type of US fighter in Britain in August was the Curtiss Mohawk, the name give to examples of the Hawk 75 taken over by the RAF after French capitulation. These too were not up to RAF standards and so were held in reserve, later serving well in both the Middle East and Far East Theaters of war.

The Defiant was fundamentally different from all the other fighters mentioned, being a two-seater with the rear gunner using a four-gun power-operated turret. Resembling a lengthened Hurricane and powered by a similar engine, it possessed a maximum speed of 488km/h (303mph). While it was unique among RAF fighters by virtue of its turret, it was also the only type without any fixed forward-firing guns.

Above: The Hurricane IIC was developed to offer even greater firepower, its fixed armament comprising four 20mm cannon and with provision for two 250lb or 500lb bombs. The mark entered RAF service from mid 1941.

Right: A Bf 109 closes in on a Spitfire in a scene played many times over during the Battle of Britain.

Below: *The unmistakable shape of the Spitfire, in this case a late Griffon-engined model with four 20mm cannon in the wing.*

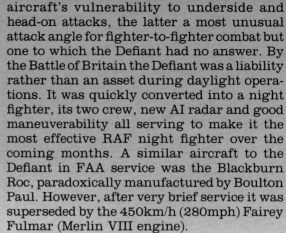

The Defiant was very new when the war broke out in 1939 and so was little known to Luftwaffe pilots when first sent into action on the continent in May 1940. This initial deployment was successful as Luftwaffe pilots maneuvered their aircraft to the rear of the Defiant believing it to be a Hurricane, a move which invited a hail of fire from the rear gunner. It was even more successful against Luftwaffe bombers, at which it could fire a 'broadside,' and by the end of the month RAF Defiants had accounted for 65 enemy destroyed. This could not last, however, and soon Luftwaffe fighter pilots realised the aircraft's vulnerability to underside and head-on attacks, the latter a most unusual attack angle for fighter-to-fighter combat but one to which the Defiant had no answer. By the Battle of Britain the Defiant was a liability rather than an asset during daylight operations. It was quickly converted into a night fighter, its two crew, new AI radar and good maneuverability all serving to make it the most effective RAF night fighter over the coming months. A similar aircraft to the Defiant in FAA service was the Blackburn Roc, paradoxically manufactured by Boulton Paul. However, after very brief service it was superseded by the 450km/h (280mph) Fairey Fulmar (Merlin VIII engine).

The RAF's main task during the Battle of Britain was to intercept Luftwaffe formations, attacking primarily the bombers. German fighter escorts were charged with defending the bombers and so most often fought fighters. This difference in emphasis between the RAF and Luftwaffe has given rise to the mistaken belief on behalf of some that Luftwaffe fighter pilots proved more successful than those of the Royal Air Force during this battle.

The very many actions of the Luftwaffe and the RAF during the Battle of Britain are too numerous to detail, and only a small number of the most significant can be mentioned here. Göring set 13 August as *Adlertag* (Eagle Day), when the Luftwaffe was to begin its heavy raids on Britain in the expectation that the RAF would be drawn into the sky for combat and ultimate destruction. This would leave the Luftwaffe free to operate over the Channel and limit attacks on German sea forces during the invasion of Britain under Operation *Sea Lion*.

Prior to *Adlertag*, Ju 87 dive bombers in

attacks on many airfields, the RAF responding to the challenge with one scramble after another. This was to be the most severe test for Dowding's élite fighter force defending Britain, facing seemingly never-ending armadas of Luftwaffe aircraft bent on wreaking destruction over the length of the country. All three Luftflotten on the Western Front were used, including Luftflotte 5 which had been formed earlier in the year and based in occupied Denmark and Norway.

Expecting to obliterate the RAF by sheer force of numbers, the Luftwaffe headed across the Channel: 72 He 111s set out for

the company of Bf 109 fighters had set out on the 8th to press home a very substantial attack on a convoy, only to be met by Hurricanes and badly mauled. On the 11th He 111s and Ju 88As raided Portland and Weymouth. The next day a large force of 63 Ju 88As struck at Ventnor on the Isle of Wight and Portsmouth, their targets being radar stations of the Chain Home system that had to be silenced if *Adlertag* was to be a success. In the event the radar at Portsmouth was badly damaged. On the same day Do 17Zs attacked the RAF station at Manston.

On 13 August several actions took place, although Göring had now decided upon the 15th for his main thrust because of bad weather. With RAF stations as the main targets, Ju 87s headed for Middle Wallop but defending Spitfires repelled the attack; 74 Do 17Zs set out for Eastchurch and Sheerness, five of those assigned to Eastchurch being lost and the Sheerness raid turned away; while Ju 88As raided Odiham and the Royal Aircraft Establishment at Farnborough. That night a highly secret attack also took place on a factory in Birmingham, the He 111 aircraft of Kampfgruppe 100 using radio-beam navigation.

The following day was not particularly active but on the 15th the Luftwaffe mounted

three RAF stations in Yorkshire, escorted by Bf 110 long-range escort fighters, while 88 Do 17Zs had Eastchurch and Rochester as their targets, the latter the home town of Short Brothers where early examples of the four-engined Stirling bomber were coming off the production lines. Seventy-five Ju 88As were assigned three targets, including the Spitfire fighter station at Middle Wallop and the Driffield Whitley bomber base. During the course of the day, the Luftwaffe found very few chinks in Britain's co-ordinated defense system. But one was certainly at Middle Wallop, where I/LG 1's Junkers caught Spitfires on the ground and wreaked much destruction. At Driffield 10 Whitleys were lost by Bomber Command, although the RAF managed to bring down six or seven Junkers, with others making a round dozen for the day. Ju 87s were not left out of the action, and 40 attacked two stations.

By sundown the fighting had ended and it was time to count the cost. The RAF, stretched to its limit, exhausted but intact, had lost 28 fighters in air combat with others damaged but repairable, and 12 pilots dead. The Luftwaffe, on the other hand, had its strength depleted by no fewer than 75 aircraft, with losses to all types that had proved to be too lightly armed to fend off the fighters and

Above: *Although the Hurricane-like appearance of the Boulton Paul Defiant initially deceived the Luftwaffe pilots into making rear attacks, the type did its best work as a night fighter.*

Right: *Groundcrew rearm a Bf 110, loading ammunition for the four 7.9mm MG 17 machine guns. The two lowered panels in the nose gave access to the ammunition feed system.*

vulnerable to anti-aircraft fire because of too little armor protection for the aircrew. The easy victories over Poland and the Low Countries had left Reichsmarschall Göring and the Luftwaffe with the unfounded belief that German aircraft, aircrew and massive strength were unchallengeable. The RAF had put the record straight.

Despite its losses the previous day, the Luftwaffe returned during daylight on the 16th and for the next month, initially in the mistaken belief that the RAF had been decimated but thereafter willing to accept the inevitable losses. But they returned without the Ju 87. Outclassed by RAF fighters and proven in the face of strong opposition to be slow, cumbersome and lacking both man- euverability and defensive firepower, 41 of its number had been lost between the 13th

and 19th and it was withdrawn from the battle to continue to fight in the Mediterran- ean, North Africa, on the Eastern Front against the Soviet Union, and elsewhere. The Ju 87 remained in use until the end of the war, though latterly mainly for night opera- tions. Other operators of the Ju 87 included the Italians.

Although several He 111 and Do 17 units were being converted to Ju 88s during 1940, the structural strength of the Dornier prob- ably made it the best Luftwaffe bomber of the Battle of Britain. On the night of 24-25 August central London got a foretaste of things to come when the Luftwaffe carried out its first such attack of the war. On 6 September Britain received a full invasion alert after air reconnaissance had shown the French Channel ports to be at a very high

Above: *With nearly 3000 warplanes at his disposal, Göring discusses tactics and receives reports on the latest victories over British aircraft.*

ing terror on London, Göring himself travelled to the Channel coast to witness the sky blackened by bombers. On the other side of the Channel RAF aircrew waited for the normal daylight raids but all was quiet. Then, as darkness began to fall, the thunderous pounding of formations of bombers was heard and London was soon ablaze.

With Britain counting its dead and wounded but not willing to give in, the bombers returned. On the 15th the Luftwaffe made its final massive assault on Britain by the light of day for, partially renewed and rested from the constant scrambles that had preceded the 7th, the RAF put up a ferocious defense and the resulting losses to the Luftwaffe were no longer acceptable. So a campaign of heavy night bombing became the Luftwaffe's order from the 16th. But Göring had failed in his most important task, to clear the skies of the RAF, and on the 17th Hitler issued the order that postponed the invasion of Britain. By its courage and tenacity over the past weeks, the RAF had saved Britain from invasion and given hope to the occupied countries of Europe. The RAF had been alone in its fight, the few against the many. Under a common banner and in a common cause, British pilots had reached for the sky in the company of Czechs, Poles, Americans, Canadians, New Zealanders, Australians, South Africans and others.

Heavy and continuous night raids by the Luftwaffe continued through September and October, forcing nearly half a million children to be evacuated from London by the 18th, but by then the Battle of Britain had been won by the RAF. Hurricane pilot Sgt J. František, a Czech with No 303 Squadron, had gained the most RAF victories with 17, followed by Plt Off E.S. Lock, a British Spitfire pilot with No 41 Squadron who managed 16 and one shared victory. The only Victoria Cross won by a pilot of Fighter Command was awarded to Flt Lt James Brindley Nicolson, a Hurricane pilot of No 249 Squadron who, though wounded, had remained in the cockpit of his burning fighter long enough to shoot down an attacking Messerschmitt Bf 110 on 16 August 1940.

Since the beginning of the campaign against Britain, the Luftwaffe had lost nearly 1800 aircraft, almost half of these Bf 109 and Bf 110 fighters. In contrast, the RAF had lost nearly 1200 fighters, of which well over 1000 had been Hurricanes and Spitfires. In many respects the RAF"s losses had been the more serious due to the much smaller size of Fighter Command compared to the massed Luftflotten of the Luftwaffe, even allowing for replacement aircraft. Had Luftwaffe operations not changed from RAF targets to civilian and from day to night when they did, despite losses, the outcome for Britain might have been different. Nobody can tell for certain. The whole history of warfare is littered with mistakes and misfortune, but the survival of Britain as an unoccupied country in 1940 was the turning point of the Western Front.

level of activity, but it was a false alarm. On 5 September a very large force of Heinkel He 111s raided London docks, while others and Do 17s bombed elsewhere *en masse*. Still Britain fought on and the Luftwaffe continued to pile up losses. But the RAF was also losing aircraft at a high rate and the situation became critical. Aircraft attrition and the loss of experienced pilots were not being made up.

Then, in one of the great blunders of the war that even rivalled Operation *Barbarossa* for unqualified bad timing, Göring turned his full rage on London and other major cities in the sure belief that the British people would buckle under the strain of sustained bombing. For the start of this new campaign, which was to begin with 625 Heinkel, Junkers, Dornier and other aircraft wreak-

CHAPTER 3

HUNTER OR HUNTED?

The Battle of Britain had been a momentous victory for the RAF, but Luftwaffe bombers and fighters continued attacks from across the Channel thereafter, with major cities taking the brunt.

In an attempt to make night bombing very accurate, German scientists had developed the early *Knickebein* and then *Gerät* systems which used high-frequency radio beams directed to cross over the exact point to be bombed. The receiver-equipped He 111s of Kampfgruppe 100, the first such pathfinder unit, had carried out the previously mentioned early trial on 13 August, but on the night of 14-15 November hundreds of bombers wreaked very severe damage to the city of Coventry, Warwickshire, the formations led by KGr 100 pathfinders using beams transmitted from the French coast. Fortunately a method of jamming the beams was discovered, forcing a change to the more sophisticated *Y-Gerät* which was also to be countered, although some successful *Gerät*-directed raids were made.

Although the RAF had begun the war with only twin-engined bombers in service, it was, unlike Germany, in the process of organizing a four-engined force. The largest of the twins in 1939-40 was the Bristol Bombay, although by then obsolete for service as a bomber on the Western Front. Designed as a bomber-transport, the 1010hp Bristol Pegasus XXII-engined Bombay had entered service in 1939 but its light 907kg (2000lb) bombload and relatively low speed of 309km/h (192mph) meant that it was used only to transport supplies to British forces in France before the Dunkirk evacuation. Other examples had been sent to the Middle East, and it was in this theater that the Bombay conducted its only bomber operations.

Bomber Command's main force in 1939-40 comprised the long-range 309km/h (192mph) Armstrong Whitworth Whitley, powered by two Armstrong Siddeley Tiger or Rolls-Royce Merlin engines and capable of carrying a 3175kg (7000lb) bombload; the uniquely-shaped Handley Page Hampden and similar Hereford medium bombers, the former using two 1000hp Bristol Pegasus XVIII engines to achieve 409km/h (254mph) and carry a 1814kg (4000lb) warload; and the long-range Vickers Wellington. The Wellington could fly at 378km/h (235mph) in

Right: *This Northrop P-61A Black Widow was one of the first 37 built; the dorsal gun turret was deleted on many subsequent production aircraft.*

Above: The Armstrong Whitworth Whitley V, a late model, joined RAF Bomber Command in August 1940.

early production form, using similar engines to those of the Hampden, but this performance was increased substantially as later versions appeared. Like the Whitley, it was fairly well armed defensively, using power-operated gun turrets in the nose and tail plus beam guns, but its warload was a little light at 2041kg (4500lbs). However, the Wellington had an important virtue other than speed.

In common with the smaller two-seat Vickers Wellesley, a 367km/h (228mph) general-purpose bomber that had entered service in 1937 but conducted most of its wartime operations against the Italians in East Africa, it employed the Vickers-developed geodetic lattice-work form of construction. This bestowed great structural strength and enabled it to sustain heavy punishment from gunfire. While the Whitley and Hampden/Hereford were dropped as pure bombers by Bomber Command during 1942, although continuing in other capacities (especially the Hampden which fought as a torpedo bomber with Coastal Command until the end of 1943), the Wellington continued in its original role until October 1943.

The earliest operations of the Whitley, Hampden and Wellington have already been mentioned, but in retaliation for German raids on central London the previous night, all three Bomber Command types were used in a raid on Berlin (the first by the RAF during this war) on the night of 25-26 August 1940. From 1941 Bomber Command gradually stepped up its offensive against the enemy, offering the only really effective way of striking at German military, industrial and city targets from isolated Britain and thus taking the war to Germany itself and other European targets until the June 1944 D-Day invasion by Allied forces.

On 1 April 1941 a Wellington was the first to drop a 4000lb 'Blockbuster' bomb, in a strike against Emden, while on the night of 30-31 May 1942 more than half the 1046 RAF bombers that attacked Cologne in the first of the famous 'Thousand-Bomber' raids were Wellingtons. Meanwhile, the pilot of one of the Hampdens that had dropped delayed-action bombs on an aqueduct of the Dortmund-Ems Canal on the night of 12-13 August 1940 had become Bomber Command's first winner of the Victoria Cross, while a radar-equipped Whitley operated by Coastal Command notched the first destruction of a German U-boat using ASV, in the Bay of Biscay on 30 November 1941. There were, of course, many more historic actions involving these aircraft in many theaters.

1942 saw the introduction of the Avro Manchester medium bomber into RAF service, its maximum speed and warload of 426km/h (265mph) and 4695kg (10,350lbs) respectively seeming to provide a very worthwhile addition to Bomber Command's strength. In fact the Manchester turned out to be a great disappointment, its 1760hp Rolls-Royce Vultures proving unreliable and forcing it out of service by mid 1942.

As every cloud is said to have a silver lining, so the failure of the Manchester was not all bad. By some redesign and increasing the wingspan to allow for four Rolls-Royce Merlin engines, the Manchester became the famous Lancaster, originally a 462km/h (287mph) bomber with a warload that could include a single 22000lb 'Grand Slam' bomb. Probably the most famous RAF bomber of the war and undoubtedly the finest, it entered RAF service in early 1942. Many Lancaster operations are legend and these include the historic attack on the Ruhr dams by No 617 Squadron led by Wg Cdr Guy Gibson, on 17-18 May 1943, using the incredible 'bouncing bombs' devised by Barnes Wallis. Another was the sinking of the German battleship *Tirpitz* in Tromso Fjord by Nos 9 and 617 Squadrons on 12 November 1944.

The Lancaster was the last of the trio of four-engined bombers that took on the brunt of Bomber Command's offensive from 1941-42. The first had been the Short Stirling, the first four-engined RAF bomber to be used in operations during World War II. The Stirling, a 418km/h (260mph) shoulder-wing aircraft powered by four 1650hp Bristol Hercules XI engines in Mk I form and carrying a 6350kg (14,000lb) bombload, undertook its first mission on the night of 10-11 February 1941, striking at Rotterdam. Between then and September 1944 Stirlings performed more than 18,400 missions but, following the arrival into service of the Halifax and Lancaster, it was slowly relegated to second-line duties.

The Halifax was a product of Handley Page, the company with the longest tradition

Below: *A Vickers Wellington III of No 419 Squadron, RAF.*

Bottom: *After the war a number of Wellington X bombers were converted into T.10 aircrew trainers. The very last Wellingtons in RAF service, each T.10 had its nose gun turret removed.*

Below: *An Avro
Lancaster I bomber of
the RAF's Battle of
Britain Memorial
Flight formates with a
Hurricane IIC (bottom)
and Spitfire PR.19.*

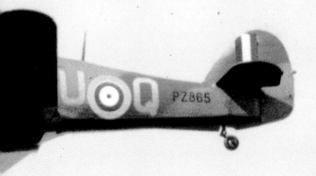

of building four-engined bombers for the RAF, dating from World War I. Serving throughout the war as a bomber (as did the Lancaster) from the time of its arrival in service in late 1940, its first mission was against targets in Le Havre on the night of 11 March 1941. Powered by four 1280hp Rolls-Royce Merlin X engines, the original Mk I version could attain a top speed of 426km/h (265mph) and carried a bombload only slightly lighter than that boasted by the Short Stirling.

Other bombers used by the RAF during World War II but supplied from the United States either by direct purchase, re-routed from occupied European countries or under Lend-Lease included Boeing B-17 Flying Fortress and Consolidated B-24 Liberator four-engined bombers, together with the twin-engined North American B-25 Mitchell, Douglas Boston, Martin Maryland/Baltimore and Martin B-26 Marauder. RAF Fortress Is (B-17Cs) undertook their first bombing mission during daylight on 8 July 1941,

attacking Wilhelmshaven. This was also the very first war mission of the B-17 in either British or US service.

The Liberator's first task with the RAF was as an anti-submarine reconnaissance bomber with Coastal Command, its very long range offering the opportunity to strike at German U-boats in mid-Atlantic. Another Consolidated aircraft, the Catalina twin-engined flying boat, was also a favorite of Coastal Command, offering greater operational endurance and hence range than even the widely acclaimed Short Sunderland long-range four-engined flying boat.

Coastal Command's regular torpedo bomber up to 1943 was the Bristol Beaufort, another descendant of the Blenheim but achieving 426km/h (265mph) on the power of its two 1130hp Bristol Taurus engines. Unlike the various models of the Blenheim, the Beaufort had a cut-down rear fuselage and a more neatly positioned dorsal gun turret. Standard armament was a 1605lb torpedo or 680kg (1500lbs) of bombs.

Above: *A four-engined Short Stirling I bomber and crew at Waterbeach in April 1942.*

Above: A Halifax 5 of No 298 Squadron at Tarrant Rushton in October 1944.

Left: Groundcrew work on the engines of a No 35 Squadron Halifax 2 at Linton-on-Ouse in 1942.

Below: A Boston III of the RAF. A number of these aircraft were diverted to the USSR as part of a continuing effort by Britain and the United States to support Soviet forces.

At sea the FAA continued to operate the Swordfish biplane until the end of the war. Its intended successor, the 259km/h (161mph) Fairey Albacore, a generally more modern biplane with enclosed accommodation, became operational in the spring of 1940 but was itself superseded by the Merlin-engined Fairey Barracuda monoplane with a top speed of 378km/h (235mph) and US-supplied Grumman Avengers (initially known in British service as Tarpons). The FAA's single-seat fighter strength on board aircraft carriers at the start of the war had comprised Sea Gladiator biplanes, but from October 1940 the US-built Grumman F4F Wildcat entered service as the Martlet, the FAA's first monoplane fighter. Slower than the Sea Hurricane that followed it into service in 1941, the Martlet was nevertheless a vitally important update and led the way for FAA carrier deployment of the F6F Hellcat as a Sea Hurricane and then Martlet replacement from 1943. The Hellcat served until the end of the war as a contemporary of the Chance Vought F4U Corsair and Supermarine's navalized Spitfire, the Seafire.

Meanwhile, the Fairey Firefly had also joined the FAA as a two-seat fighter-reconnaissance aircraft in 1943, the Rolls-Royce Griffon engine of early versions bestowing a speed of 509km/h (316mph). Armed with four forward-firing cannon and with provision for rockets and bombs, the Firefly was used mainly against the Japanese.

Left: *North American Mitchell 2s flown by No 180 Squadron, RAF, at Foulsham in July 1943.*

Left: *Grumman Avenger Is of No 846 Squadron, FAA, photographed in December 1943.*

Right: *Groundcrew prepare to attach an 18-inch torpedo to a Fairey Albacore biplane of the Fleet Air Arm.*

Above: *This Fleet Air Arm Fairey Barracuda 2 carries a 1620lb torpedo.*

Left: *Bristol Beaufort torpedo bombers of No 217 Squadron, RAF, make a low-level sweep.*

Left: From 1944 Fleet Air Arm Martlet fighters were renamed Wildcats, a name used by the US Navy. This Wildcat V of No 882 Squadron is about to take off from HMS Searcher in 1944.

Below: A surviving Grumman Martlet I pictured in the FAA Museum at Yeovilton. Ordered as one of a batch of 30 (five of which went to Canada), it arrived in Britain in July 1940.

Above: *Westland's greatest contribution to the war effort was undoubtedly the Lysander, an Army co-operation aircraft carrying four guns and with provision for six light bombs but also remembered for taking British agents into enemy-held territory with the Special Air Service.*

Left: *A Fairey Firefly two-seat fighter-reconnaissance aircraft, photographed in May 1944.*

With the intention of providing the RAF with its first ever single-seat but twin-engined fighter, Westland had produced a design pre-war which became the Whirlwind. An entirely new concept, it achieved 579km/h (360mph) on the power of two 885hp Rolls-Royce Peregrine I engines and boasted the lethal firepower of four nose-mounted cannon. Trials showed the fighter to be at its best at low level and it was employed from late 1940 as a bomber escort, accompanying fast light bombers during attacks on German targets. But various mechanical problems with the engines showed themselves, and the fighter's high landing speed (caused by the deletion of Handley Page leading-edge slats) forced careful selection of airfields from which Whirlwinds could operate. As the result of these and other factors, production was restricted to just 112 of the 400 aircraft

ordered. From the late summer of 1942 Whirlwinds were no longer viewed as suitable escort fighters, their excellent maneuverability not overcoming the performance fall-off at high altitude, and so remaining aircraft were converted into fighter-bombers with the intention of allowing them to strike Channel and continental targets hard, fast and low. By 1943, however, the Whirlwind had been withdrawn, leaving the Lysander army co-operation aircraft to remain Westland's most important contribution to the wartime RAF.

Across the Atlantic, Lockheed had used the single-seat, twin-engined formula to produce the P-38 Lightning, although in general configuration it was entirely different to the Whirlwind and adopted twin booms to support the tail unit. Larger, much more powerful and with a higher service ceiling, the Lightning was deployed widely by the USAAF in the Pacific Theater, North Africa and in the UK, but early examples of the Lightning intended for the RAF proved underpowered and lacked superchargers and the fighter was thus initially rejected for British use.

Far more significant to the RAF were the two-seat twin-engined fighters, like the Beaufighter already mentioned. Another was the Mosquito, de Havilland's 'wooden wonder.' One of Britain's finest warplanes of World War II, the Mosquito had been conceived in the pre-war period as a very fast light bomber, constructed almost entirely of wood and using fabric-covered plywood as the skin. Adopting two high-powered Rolls-Royce Merlin engines, it was intended to be armed only with an offensive load, relying on speed for its defense against enemy attack. Begun as a company venture, rejected for

development by the wartime Ministry of Aircraft Production and then accepted, the first prototype flew on 25 November 1940. It immediately became clear that the Mosquito was no ordinary warplane – indeed, it was so fast that reconnaissance and fighter prototypes were put in hand at once.

In 1941 the most urgent need was for a high-speed reconnaissance aircraft and so the very first Mosquitos in RAF service were Mk I photographic reconnaissance aircraft, which began operating in daylight over France in September 1941. These easily escaped Luftwaffe interceptors. The first armed variant was the Mk IV, a light bomber capable of 612km/h (380mph) on the power of two 1250hp Merlin 21s. Carrying a 907kg (2000lb) bombload but no guns, it was first used (on 31 May 1942) against a target in Cologne and this represented the very first

Right: A line-up of Focke-Wulf Fw 200 Condor long-range maritime reconnaissance bombers.

Below: The first production Lockheed P-38, which was delivered to the RAF in December 1941 as a Lightning I. To its rear stand long-range examples of the Hudson III.

daylight attack by the speedy Mosquito, against which the Germans had little reply. One of the most famous Mosquito bomber sorties was undertaken on 25 September 1942 when aircraft of No 105 Squadron (the RAF's first Mosquito bomber unit) attacked the Gestapo headquarters in Oslo, Norway, flying at extremely low altitude to remain undetected.

On 30 January 1943 No 105 Squadron carried out the first daylight attack on Berlin, and many other actions followed. However, in April 1942 the Mosquito fighter had begun operations, first as a radar-equipped night fighter superseding the Beaufighter and later as a day and night fighter-bomber and anti-shipping aircraft. The initial version was the Mk II night fighter, capable of a stunning 595km/h (370mph). However, it was in Mk VI form that the Mosquito fighter was most widely flown. A fighter-bomber with similar engines to the Mk IV, and similar top speed, it was armed with the devastating combination of four cannon and four machine guns plus two 250lb or 500lb bombs in the fuselage bay and two more bombs or rockets under the wing.

Probably the most famous action of the Mosquito fighter-bomber was that on 18 February 1944, when 19 aircraft flew a daring mission to breach the German prison at Amiens, liberating members of the Resistance awaiting execution. In April 1944 Mk VIs destroyed German records at The Hague giving details of members of the Dutch Resistance, thus saving many lives. In another

field of operations, just prior to that April raid, a navalized Mosquito had landed on board HMS *Indefatigable*, the first FAA twin-engined aircraft to make a carrier landing. Mosquitos were also particularly useful against the menace of the V-1 flying-bomb: a reconnaissance Mosquito first photographed a V-1 at the highly secret German rocket establishment at Peenemunde in October 1943, Mosquito bombers pounded V-1 sites during the summer of 1944, and Mosquito fighters shot down airborne V-1s as they headed towards their British targets.

The Mosquito proved equally effective in other wartime theaters, whether against the Italians over the Mediterranean, in North Africa or fighting the Japanese in Burma, where fighter-bomber Mosquitos took over from US-built Vultee Vengeance two-seat dive bombers and Blenheim Vs.

For long-range fighter-bomber missions there was little to better twin-engined aircraft, but single-seat and single-engined fighters were still required in huge numbers for other missions. By 1942 Hawker Hurricanes were of little use as fighters against the Luftwaffe, except at sea on board aircraft carriers; offering fighter cover for convoys was particularly useful during 1942, especially for the convoys sailing through the Arctic Ocean to the Soviet Union where they helped counter the threat from Luftwaffe maritime aircraft of the Blohm und Voss Bv 138 and Focke-Wulf Fw 200 types. Hawker's follow-on fighter to the Hurricane was the Typhoon, designed to use the 24-cylinder Napier Sabre engine and first flown

Above: *Eight 60lb rockets are fitted to a wing leader's de Havilland Mosquito VI at Banff in 1945.*

Right: *A Gloster-built example of the Hawker Typhoon IB in flight.*

as a prototype in February 1940. Although expected to be in service later that year, initial deployment did not take place until September of the following year.

Nevertheless, with a speed of 663km/h (412mph) from a 2180hp Sabre II engine, it appeared that the wait would be worthwhile. Either armed with 12 machine guns or, later, four cannon, the Typhoon looked set to counter a new German threat that had proved beyond the existing versions of the Spitfire. Back in June 1939, the first flight had taken place of a new German fighter, the Focke-Wulf Fw 190. Unlike most fighters under development at that time, it used a radial engine. This was a BMW 18-cylinder double-row engine driving a three-blade propeller with large spinner, offering a smaller drag-inducing frontal area on the Fw 190 than had been usual for radial-engined fighters up to that time.

An extremely clean-looking single-seater, the Fw 190 first went to II/JG 26 which had been operating in France with Bf 109Es. This was in July 1941. Quite how good an aircraft the Fw 190 was was quickly demonstrated. In February 1941 the RAF had received its first production Spitfire V, the fighter-bomber version intended for home and overseas operations and to make sweeping attacks on German targets over the Channel. By no means slow, with a top speed of 602km/h (374mph), it was this version that first engaged the Fw 190 while operating over the French coast in early September. In the ensuing combat, four Fw 190As destroyed three Spitfires and scattered the rest – and this at an altitude of about 4000m (13,100ft) which most suited the Spitfire.

The Fw 190 was capable of speeds ranging from 626km/h (389mph) to more than 644km/h (400mph) in initial A-series form, on the power of the BMW 801D engine, and proved superior to the Spitfire V in all but turning circle and service ceiling. Fw 190s

were subsequently built in fighter and fighter-bomber versions, the Fw 190F also operating from 1943 in the close-support role as successor to the hopelessly outdated Ju 87. The fastest version that became operational was the Fw 190D-9, capable of 686km/h (426mph) from a 1776hp Junkers Jumo 213A-1 engine, though much higher speeds were managed by versions under development. As a fighter-bomber, the Fw 190D had two fewer cannon than the A-series, with two cannon and two machine guns, although armament was supplemented by a 500kg bomb.

Though the Fw 190 operated on the Eastern Front against Soviet forces, in Italy and over the Mediterranean, its main wartime tasks were to raid the southern coast of Britain and intercept Allied fighters and bombers over occupied Europe. It was to counter Fw 190 raids that the Hawker Typhoon had been developed. Once in RAF

Below: Armorers work on a Hawker Typhoon IB of No 257 Squadron, RAF, at Warmwell in May 1943.

service, however, the Typhoon's Sabre engine not only proved unreliable but failed to give the fighter anything like an adequate high-altitude performance or rate of climb.

Fortunately, many Fw 190 sweeps over the Channel were at low altitude, at which height the Typhoon proved superior. By July 1942 new Spitfire IXs had been deployed by the RAF, the first 400mph-plus version in service. Together, the Typhoon and Spitfire IX met the challenge of the Fw 190, although the Fw 190 still had many performance advantages over the Spitfire.

Like the Fw 190 and the Hurricane 'Hurri-bomber,' the Typhoon had been designed to be capable of carrying bombs, and before the end of the year Typhoons were flying strike missions against shipping targets in the Channel and over occupied Europe. This type of warfare was to prove rewarding for the Typhoon, which quickly earned a reputation as a uniquely skilled trainbuster. Eventually carrying up to two 1000lb bombs or eight large rocket projectiles, the Typhoon created havoc with German communications, armor and airfields. Following the D-Day landings in mid 1944, Typhoons blasted German armor at the instruction of ground forces, waves of aircraft decimating Panzer divisions as they retreated.

Refinement of the Typhoon design led to the Tempest V, the only version of this new fighter-bomber to see wartime action. Still using a 2180hp Sabre II engine and featuring the Typhoon-type chin radiator airscoop, the Tempest V adopted a new semi-elliptical thin-section wing of slightly increased span instead of the Typhoon's thick straight-tapering wing, and a redesigned fin. One problem with the design was a lack of room to house substantial wing tanks, a problem resolved by lengthening the fuselage to accommodate fuel. The bubble-style cockpit canopy of late Typhoons was adopted as standard for the Tempest. Only marginally heavier empty than the Typhoon but with cleaner aerodynamics, the Tempest V managed 687km/h (427mph) and greatly extended range. Tempests flew alongside Typhoons during the Allied push into Europe from 1944 and proved highly successful destroyers of V-1 flying bombs.

However, some of the most memorable actions began in the autumn of 1944, when Tempest Vs and Spitfire XIVs were assigned the task of defending the British-held Nijmegen bridge against Luftwaffe attack. Among the German aircraft bombing the area were the Luftwaffe's first turbojet-powered warplanes, Messerschmitt Me 262s and perhaps Arado Ar 234 Blitz bombers, the latter arriving in the area in November. Although finding it extremely difficult to counter the Me 262s as they made their diving runs to the target, thereafter pulling away at very great speed, both types of British aircraft managed to bring down some jets. A version of the Tempest intended for operation against the Japanese was the Mk II, a still faster aircraft using a powerful Bristol Centaurus radial engine. Of much neater appearance, production examples appeared from October 1944 but none were in service by VJ-Day.

Hawker had already designed its successor to the Tempest, the Fury, to a 1943 specification. Like the Tempest II, it used a Centaurus radial engine – and, although it was not required by the RAF, a version was built for service with the FAA as the Sea Fury. First flown in February 1945, it did not enter service until two years after the end of the war. A similar fate attended the Blackburn Firebrand, intended to be a four-cannon fighter with the FAA and first flown in early 1942 but later assigned the role of torpedo-carrying strike aircraft. The Firebrand did not enter service until September 1945.

Meanwhile, since 1942 Britain and the Empire had not been alone in the fight against the Axis powers of Germany and Italy. Following the Japanese naval attack on Pearl Harbor on 7 December 1941 (see *One Day In December*), the US had declared war on Japan on the 8th, with Britain following suit. Three days later both Germany and Italy declared war on the United States, with the US responding. By February 1942 the USAAF had established a European operations headquarters in Britain: a decision had been made to fight in the Pacific against the Japanese and in the west against Germany and Italy simultaneously, with the defeat of Germany as the main priority. By July the first four-engined bombers to equip the USAAF in Europe began arriving, the B-17s

Below: *The Douglas A-20 Havoc served the US Army Air Force in Europe, the Far East and North Africa.*

landing at Prestwick. However, even before these were ready for operational use, USAAF crews of the 15th Bombardment Squadron used RAF Douglas Boston light bombers to attack German airfields in Holland. This, the USAAF's first bombing missions over Europe of the war, significantly took place on 4 July. A-20 Havoc bombers, similar to the Bostons, were subsequently used by the USAAF in Europe, the Far East and North Africa.

A most important date in the annals of the USAAF was 17 August 1942. On that day B-17s of the 97th Bombardment Group attacked the Rouen-Scotteville marshalling yards in France, the first heavy raid in Europe by the USAAF. The B-17, Boeing's Flying Fortress, was to become perhaps the most famous wartime bomber of any nation. First flown as a prototype on 28 July 1935, the initial B-17B production model appeared shortly before the war in Europe began. The RAF received some of the earliest aircraft as Fortress Is, similar to B-17Cs with machine gun armament increased from five to seven

Below: *Early production Boeing B-17B Flying Fortresses, delivered to the USAAC between late 1939 and April 1940. Note the gun blisters on the fuselage sides and the dorsal blister for the navigator, both features of this model.*

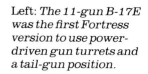

Left: *The 11-gun B-17E was the first Fortress version to use power-driven gun turrets and a tail-gun position.*

Below: *B-17Gs of the US 8th Air Force over England. The 'G' was the version that introduced the remotely-controlled Bendix chin gun turret to the Flying Fortress.*

Below: *B-17E Yankee takes on fuel from a tanker. Note the manned ventral ball turret, introduced on this version.*

and with later mark 1200hp Wright R-1820 engines. When the B-17 was found to be lacking in defensive armament and armor plating following missions in Europe by the RAF in July 1941, Boeing incorporated self-sealing fuel tanks and improved armor protection in the follow-up B-17D version for the USAAF, that service's B-17Cs being modernized to this standard. Almost all the small number of B-17Ds built were based in the Philippines at the time of the Japanese attack and many were destroyed, other early B-17s having been destroyed at Pearl Harbor.

The B-17E represented the first major production version, serving mainly with the USAAF but also with the RAF as the Fortress IIA and incorporating (for the first time) power-operated gun turrets. Powered, like the 'C', by R-1820-65 radial engines, the B-17E could fly at 510km/h (317mph). It possessed a range of 3219km (2000 miles) and carried 11 machine guns for defense.

The RAF also received the Fortress II, the British equivalent of the B-17F that was the first version to be built in thousands.

The most important version of the B-17 was the B-17G, also used by the RAF as the Fortress III. Armed with 13 machine guns and carrying up to 7983kg (17,600lbs) of bombs – although a much smaller load was normal to maintain an adequate range – it had a top speed of 426km/h (287mph) on its four 1200hp R-1820-97 engines. This was easily the heaviest Fortress version. Total B-17 production was 12,731, with Boeing's Seattle factory alone producing 16 a day at its peak. Some were subsequently converted to other versions.

With many USAAF bombers based in Britain, a 24-hour bombing campaign of German targets began, with the USAAF

taking on daylight raids and the RAF attacking by night. As a consequence, US losses were the more severe, although the tactic enabled great pressure to be applied on Germany. Although Consolidated B-24 Liberators were used most widely in the Pacific – with 22 December 1942 marking the first major raid on a Japanese airfield in the Central Pacific by the USAAF's 307th Bombardment Group – the type was also active in Europe and elsewhere.

Following the January 1943 decision by Churchill, Roosevelt and military leaders to invade Sicily as a first step into Europe before any major cross-Channel invasion, bombers began a softening-up campaign of Sicily, Sardinia and Italy. However, even before this, on 4 December 1942, Liberators of the 9th Air Force had bombed Naples, the first USAAF raid on Italy.

From November 1944 the Douglas A-26 Invader joined the USAAF in Europe, then the Pacific, using six or eight nose guns, dorsal-turret guns and up to 1814kg (4000lbs) of bombs or rockets to press home attacks. The Martin B-26 Marauder, which had first seen action in the Pacific, had earlier joined European squadrons of the US Eighth

Above: *Consolidated B-24 Liberators of the US 8th Air Force head out from England on a daylight mission over enemy territory, escorted by P-51 Mustang fighters.*

Left: *Princess (later Queen) Elizabeth names a USAAF B-17, Rose of York.*

Right: *Liberators served with distinction over Europe as well as in the Pacific.*

and Ninth Air Forces in May 1943.

Heavy bombing of targets in Europe had shown the need for long-range fighters to escort bombers all the way to and from targets and so reduce losses through enemy interception. The USAAF was especially vulnerable because of its daylight missions. The Lockheed P-38 Lightning was an answer, and indeed was initially deployed by the USAAF in Europe in the late summer of 1942 before going also to the Pacific and North Africa. Although its range was really too short to provide an entirely satisfactory solution, it was nevertheless a welcome sight for B-17 and B-24 crews on missions over occupied Europe.

From May 1943 B-17s and B-24s got a new escort in the form of the mighty Republic P-47 Thunderbolt. Developed from the Seversky P-35, of which small numbers were in the Philippines when the Japanese attacked, and the Republic P-43 Lancer which also saw very limited action against the Japanese, the Thunderbolt first flew as a prototype on 6 May 1941. One of the outstanding fighters of the war, more than 15,000 were eventually built. P-47s served first with the USAAF in Europe, then in the Pacific with the USAAF and later the RAF, the Mediterranean and other areas, a number also going to the Soviet Union under US Lend-Lease arrangements.

The first model in Europe was the eight-gun P-47B, a huge tubby fighter with a 2000hp Pratt & Whitney R-2800 radial engine. In service it was shown to lack maneuverability, but this was compensated

Left: *A Martin B-26B Marauder of the 596th Bombardment Squadron, USAAF, pictured in August 1944.*

Right: *A Republic P-47C Thunderbolt of the 56th Fighter Group prepares to escort B-17s on a day mission from England.*

Below: *The first Douglas A-26 Invader runs up its engines before flight.*

for by a top speed of 663km/h (412mph). Range was also found wanting for bomber escort duties. Luckily, the most important of all versions built was just around the corner; the P-47D became operational in late 1943. Powered by a 2300hp R-2800-59 (or similar) radial engine, the P-47D could fly at 687km/h (427mph) but, more importantly, had a strengthened wing to support auxiliary fuel tanks or bombs. The fastest version was the P-47N, capable of 752km/h (467mph) and possessing very long range. Two P-47Ds claimed the first ever jet fighter shot down by the USAAF, when on 28 August 1944 the 78th Fighter Group claimed a

Messerschmitt Me 262A-2a of KG 51 Kommando Schenk that had been operating out of Juvincourt.

Me 262s were also victims of the famous North American P-51 Mustang, a single-seat fighter of even greater fame than the Thunderbolt. Although most often associated with the USAAF during World War II, the Mustang was in fact designed to an order of the British Purchasing Commission. The prototype flew on the power of a 1100hp Allison V-1710 inline engine for the first time on 26 October 1940 and production P-51s entered service with the RAF as Mustang Is in April 1942. Though managing

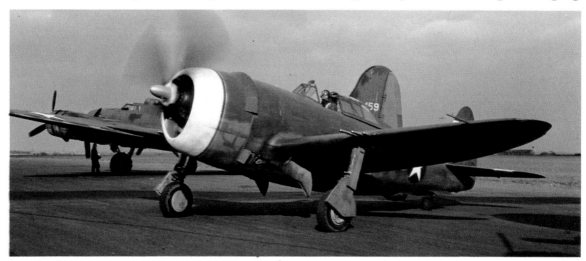

Below: *The Lockheed P-38J featured an air intake in each engine cowling to provide cooling for the oil radiator and intercooler. The aircraft pictured (foreground) is accompanied by an F-5B photographic reconnaissance Lightning.*

Above: *Early version P-51 Mustangs are pictured here in USAAF service.*

Inset top right: *Lt Darwin L Berry in his P-51D based in England.*

628km/h (390mph) and possessing good range – indeed, it was superior in speed and range to any contemporary RAF fighter – the Mustang had disappointing high-altitude performance, making it unsuited to bomber escort duties. Therefore, the Mustang I and similar Mustang II, both carrying eight guns, together with the four-cannon Mustang IA, were assigned fighter-reconnaissance roles. Similar fighters were received by the USAAF.

In Britain a small number of Mustangs had been fitted experimentally with Rolls-Royce Merlin engines, which transformed the fighter's performance from reasonable to

extraordinary. From February 1944 the RAF deployed the Mustang III and then IV, fitted with Packard-built Merlin V-1650 engines of 1680hp and with a top speed of 711km/h (442mph). With extra fuel and underwing stores-carrying capability, the Mustang had arrived in its most deadly forms, the USAAF also taking the similar P-51B, C, D and K. The Mustang IV/P-51D and K were the first versions to change over from a faired to a bubble-type cockpit canopy. Whether escorting bombers or destroying V-1s, striking as a fighter-bomber in Europe or in other theaters, or used on high-speed reconnaissance sorties, the P-51 proved outstanding.

Left: A Mustang I of
No 2 Squadron, the
first RAF unit to use the
fighter, based at
Sawbridgeworth and
just operational in July
1942.

With the development of the first 'super-bomber,' the Boeing B-29 Superfortress, a new type of escort fighter was required. One solution proposed led to the P-82 Twin Mustang, literally two P-51s joined by a common center wing and tailplane. First flown in 1945, none entered operational service before the end of the war.

Another important American aircraft manufacturer at the outbreak of war in Europe was Northrop, although the only aircraft from this company to see action in the early war years were a few DB-8A-3N (A-17 derivative) attack monoplanes in the hands of the Netherlands and two dozen N-3PB convoy escort, anti-submarine and re-connaissance floatplanes used by the RAF's No 330 Squadron, manned by Norwegians and flying out of Iceland. In contrast to these unremarkable aircraft, Northrop's other combat plane of World War II was stunning. Some 11 months before America joined the war, the USAAC had ordered prototypes of the first-ever purpose-designed and radar-equipped US night fighter, the Northrop P-61 Black Widow. A menacing-looking aircraft, it carried radar in a long nose without obstructing armament, the pilot occupying a forward cockpit and the stepped

rear cabin accommodating the two remaining crew members. Twin engined and twin boomed, all production versions carried four cannon in a ventral position, early and late examples also having four-gun remotely-controlled dorsal turrets. The P-61B ex-panded into intruder roles by virtue of underwing hardpoints for bombs. The P-61B became the most important version of the Black Widow. Powered by two 2000hp Pratt & Whitney R-2800 radial engines, it could attain 590km/h (366mph). Although built in hundreds rather than thousands, the P-61 proved itself a very useful addition to US squadrons fighting in the Pacific from mid 1944, and was also employed with success on the Western Front.

Surprisingly few entirely new warplanes joined the Luftwaffe after the early battles of World War II had been fought, leading to the conclusion that too much reliance was placed on warplanes of pre-war appearance. Throughout the war the Luftwaffe lacked adequate four-engined bombers, while bombers in service made too little use of power-controlled gun turrets and turrets in the extreme tail. Complacency over existing aircraft was caused in part by the leaders of the Third Reich expecting to overwhelm

Above: *The North American P-82 Twin Mustang, together with the German Heinkel He 111Z, was one of the few 'twinned' aircraft of the war.*

Right: *Northrop P-61 Black Widow night fighters without dorsal turrets. The turret was subsequently re-adopted on the production line.*

Above: *A Dornier Do 217K-2 with the later bulbous, unstepped forward fuselage.*

Below: *A Junkers Ju 188 abandoned (with sundry fighters) on an airfield at Erfurt, Germany, stripped of an engine and all armament, though the gunsight for the 20mm MG 151 nose cannon is still visible.*

Britain in 1940. With this in mind, there appeared little point in rushing forward with the development of new aircraft for service in years ahead when derivatives of existing warplanes would do the job, notwithstanding Germany's designs on the Soviet Union. War with the US was not a factor in 1939 – but within three weeks of the US entry and nine days after that country declared war on Germany, the German Air Ministry had initiated the *Amerika-Bomber* program.

Prewar, Dornier had offered an export version of the Do 17 as the Do 215. With orders from Yugoslavia and Sweden, it went into production with two 1075hp Daimler-Benz DB 610A engines but, before any could be delivered, exports were blocked and pro-

duction aircraft taken over by the Luftwaffe. This service received Do 215B-1 reconnaissance-bombers, carrying 1000kg (2205lbs) of bombs and cameras, and reconnaissance Do 215B-4s. Their service life was short, extending only from February 1940 to 1942. Some aircraft were converted into Do 215B-5 intruders and night fighters, with radar antenna carried on a new solid nose in which were two cannon and four machine guns.

Even before the Do 215 demonstrators had picked up foreign orders, Dornier had flown (in August 1938) a new and more powerful bomber as the Do 217. Centered on the use of two 1580hp BMW 801 radial engines, small numbers of early production Do 217A reconnaissance aircraft and Do 217C bombers

were followed by the major version, the Do 217E with a deeper fuselage. Although some examples were delivered to the Luftwaffe with unique tail-cones that opened umbrella fashion to act as dive brakes for dive-bomber operations, 'Es' delivered from late 1940 were used mainly for reconnaissance, bombing and anti-shipping missions, while in 1942 some were converted into Do 217J night fighters and intruder aircraft. The first action by a Do 217 night fighter took place in May 1943. A derivative of the Do 217J with 1750hp DB 603A engines was the Do 217N, capable of 515km/h (320mph).

The final two heavy bomber variants of the Do 217 were the Do 217K and M, powered by BMW 801D and DB 603A engines respectively. These two versions differed from all others, with the exception of the Do 217P reconnaissance aircraft, by having new forward fuselage sections with completely rounded, glazed noses. The Do 217M carried six machine guns for defense, including one in an electrically operated dorsal turret, and

Below: *Luftwaffe groundcrew arm a Heinkel He 111 before operations.*

Above: *The Heinkel He 115 seaplane could, according to version, attain speeds of up to 355km/h (221mph) and played a major part in the harassment of shipping in the English Channel during 1940 and thereafter.*

Left: *A Heinkel He 59 torpedo-bomber and reconnaissance biplane at its mooring.*

4000kg (8820lbs) of bombs.

Interestingly, versions of the Do 217 were among the first aircraft equipped to carry and launch missiles. In August 1943 the Luftwaffe's II/KG 100, flying the Do 217E-5, began anti-shipping attacks on Allied vessels in the Bay of Biscay, launching rocket-powered and remotely-controlled Henschel Hs 293A-1s. HMS *Egret* was sunk by such a missile on 27 August. On 9 September Do 217K-2s from III/KG 100 succeeded in sinking the Italian warship *Roma*, using Ruhrstahl/Kramer *Fritz X-1* missiles, as it sailed with other ships to be surrendered to the Allies. In the same group of warships was the *Italia*, which was damaged by a similar air-launched missile.

Junkers faced the more difficult task of producing a successor to its highly successful and massively produced Ju 88. The chosen power plant for the Ju 188 was the 1776hp Junkers Jumo 213A, but shortages made it necessary to fit early examples with less powerful BMW 801s. Externally, the Ju 188 differed from the Ju 88 in having a very different nose section, in which the Ju 88's stepped nose was replaced by a bulbous, heavily-glazed nose of a type not dissimilar to that used by the Dornier Do 217, while pointed tips to the wing provided the other recognition point.

Initial production Ju 188Es first entered service with I/KG 6 in October 1943. Eventually, models were produced for bombing, reconnaissance and torpedo-bomber roles. Total production of the Ju 188 was tiny when compared to the Ju 88, a night-fighter

variant having been abandoned as it proved no better than the existing Ju 88 in this role. The Ju 188E-1 bomber carried one cannon and three machine guns for defense and an offensive load of up to 3000kg (6614lbs) of bombs. Maximum speed was 500km/h (311mph), this being only a little slower than the Ju 188A-2.

Variants of the Ju 188 intended for operation at very high altitudes had led to the development of pressurized models, but few came from the factory and it is probable that none entered Luftwaffe service. However, a new pressurized warplane was proposed as the Ju 388, intended as a radar-equipped high-altitude fighter, bomber and reconnaissance type. In the event, the only version to see any operational service worth recording was the Ju 388L reconnaissance aircraft. Had the Ju 388K bomber achieved substantial operational use it would have proven a devastating warplane, possessing a speed of 610km/h (379mph) on the power of a pair of 1880hp BMW engines.

In addition to its He 111, Heinkel had achieved early success with the He 115 twin-float seaplane, employed as a torpedo bomber and for other maritime roles. Although remaining in service until the summer of 1944, it had really had its day by 1942. Another twin-engined BMW-powered Heinkel maritime aircraft of the early war years was the He 59, a large biplane that had first entered service in 1935. Its poor top speed of 220km/h (137mph) made it of little use, except for coastal patrol work after the 1940 German invasion of the Low Countries.

Prior to World War II Heinkel had begun development of a four-engined heavy bomber as the He 177 Greif, its maiden flight occurring on 19 November 1939. Had the He 177 achieved its goals it would have given the Allies new headaches. As it was, the only long-range four-engined heavy bomber to become fully operational with the Luftwaffe during World War II was a failure.

With the He 177, Heinkel had abided by the German Air Ministry's insistence that it be suitable for bombing, anti-shipping and dive-bombing roles, and that high speed was to be achieved by keeping within strict weight limits. Heinkel produced a mid-wing bomber in which pairs of Daimler-Benz DB 601 engines were coupled to form 2700hp DB 606s, each pair driving a single four-blade propeller. Well armed defensively, with a machine gun in the nose, one machine gun in a remotely-controlled dorsal position, two machine guns and a cannon in a ventral gondola and a machine gun in the extreme tail, it could carry a warload of up to 6000kg (13,230lbs) over short ranges or 2000kg (4410lbs) over an impressive range of up to 5600km (3480 miles).

Put into service before problems with engine overheating and structural weakness had been resolved, the 490km/h (304mph) bomber was first flown in action on the Eastern Front during the winter of 1942-43 but several of the early machines were lost to fires caused by the engine arrangement. The He 177 soon earned the nickname 'Flaming Coffin.' He 177s were also operated against shipping in the Atlantic and Mediterranean and a small number participated in the 'Little Blitz' bombing raids of early 1944, the first

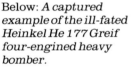

Below: *A captured example of the ill-fated Heinkel He 177 Greif four-engined heavy bomber.*

on London taking place on 21 January that year. Fewer and fewer He 177 operations were conducted towards the end of the war as fuel shortages and maintenance problems kept them grounded. Had the engine problems been resolved, however – perhaps with a more conventional engine arrangement as used by Allied bombers – the He 177 could have offered the Luftwaffe a much-needed long-range strategic weapon.

Heinkel's disappointment in not getting its He 100 and He 112 single-seat fighters into prewar Luftwaffe service, despite German propaganda to the contrary, meant that virtually all the company's contributions to the war effort over the ensuing years were bombers or their variants. There were, however, two notable exceptions. One was the He 219 Uhu (Owl), an unusual two-seater capable of 670km/h (416mph) in its most important He 219A-7 form, flying on the power of two 1900hp Daimler-Benz DB 603 engines. Operated as a night fighter from April 1943 but with major service beginning in the following year, it was one of the few aircraft capable of dealing with the high-speed RAF Mosquito. Armament of the He 219A-7 was six forward-firing and two rear-mounted cannon. Unfortunately for Heinkel, the subsequent shortage of engines and the necessity to produce large quantities of fighters to defend Germany from Allied bomber attack meant that the production of twin-engined fighters had to give way to single-seaters. Therefore, despite its excellence, fewer than 270 examples of the Uhu were completed.

Messerschmitt had begun the development of a Bf 110 replacement prior to hostilities,

and the prototype Me 210 flew for the first time in early September 1939. Like its predecessor, it was a twin-engined two-seater, the various production models which followed all using 1350hp Daimler-Benz DB 601F engines. Intended for the heavy fighter and dive-bomber roles, the Me 210 proved capable of 620km/h (385mph) and could carry up to 1000kg (2205lbs) of bombs in addition to its other armament of two cannon and two machine guns firing forward and remotely-controlled rear-firing machine guns. Unfortunately for Messerschmitt, the Me 210 was not a good warplane and was prone to spin out of control. Although declared little suited to operational service, Me 210s appeared on the Eastern Front from the winter of 1941 and over the UK from September 1942, by which time the type had already been taken out of production.

Below: Heinkel's He 219 Uhu two-seat fighter, seen here in A-5/R1 form, was an effective combat aircraft, but too few were available to alter the course of the air war in Europe.

Right: *A
Messerschmitt
Me 410A-1 Hornisse
heavy fighter, pictured
in 1943.*

Messerschmitt had attempted to redeem its reputation by proposing the Me 310 as a pressurized and modified derivative of the Me 210, but this was not selected for production. Instead the Me 410 was put into service. This was basically an Me 210 with the 1750hp DB 603A engines driving four-blade propellers, featuring also longer engine cowlings, a revised wing, flaps and ailerons, and incorporating the deeper rear fuselage of development Me 210s. This was a far better warplane, capable of 625km/h (388mph) and carrying the forward-firing armament of four cannon and two machine guns. In the hands of V/KG 2, Me 410s first went into action over the UK in mid 1943 and proved a match for the best RAF defenders by day or, more usually, by night. Production of the Me 410 was several times that of the Me 210 but still amounted to fewer than 1200 examples.

Unlike Messerschmitt, which produced no operational single-engined fighter to follow the Bf 109, Focke-Wulf developed the Ta 152 to follow its Fw 190. Based upon the Fw 190, the Ta 152 (first flown in July 1944) was planned with various engine and wingspan combinations according to the intended role. Designed principally as a high-altitude interceptor with a pressurized cockpit to

Above: *Hitler's
Volksjäger (People's
Fighter), the Heinkel
He 162 Salamander,
carried its single
turbojet engine above
the fuselage in the style
of the V-1 flying bomb.*

attack high-flying Allied heavy bombers, the only version to enter Luftwaffe service and see some action was the Ta 152H-1, powered by a Junkers Jumo 213E-1 engine giving a rating of 2050hp with methanol-water injection at take-off. Capable of 760km/h (472mph) at high altitude with nitrous oxide injection for the engine and using a widespan wing, it was used in the closing stages of the war as an airfield-defense fighter and ground-attack aircraft.

Three nations – namely Britain, Germany and the US – developed jet fighters during World War II, of which those of Britain and Germany were deployed operationally. How-

ever, Germany was alone in the deployment of a rocket-powered interceptor and a jet bomber. Two German manufacturing companies were paramount in the development of the fighters – Heinkel and Messerschmitt. The former, having produced the first ever specifically-designed and piloted rocket plane as the experimental He 176 (which first flew on 20 June 1939) and the first turbojet-powered aeroplane as the He 178 (flown initially on 27 August the same year), was unsuccessful in getting its twin-turbojet He 280 fighter into production. Despite its extensive prewar and wartime research into rocket motors and turbojet engines, Heinkel

had to content itself with the He 162 Salamander as its only production turbojet fighter to see active service. The *Volksjäger* (People's Fighter), as it was also known, was a last-ditch aircraft, intended to stave off the massive Allied bomber formations flying over Germany by the summer of 1944, to be built by semi-skilled labor overseeing unskilled workers using available materials and only one engine. Yet it was to fly at a minimum of 750km/h (466mph), was expected to be built in vast quantities and piloted by members of the Hitler Youth previously trained only on gliders.

The first He 162 prototype flew on 6 December 1944, within 90 days of the project's conception. Despite many problems, which had included structural failure of the wooden wing on the first prototype and being a particularly unpleasant aircraft to fly, the Salamander entered production. However, manufacture was slow and the few operational aircraft were manned only by fully-qualified Luftwaffe pilots. Capable of 840km/h (522mph) on the power of a BMW 003E engine rated at 800kg (1764lbs) static thrust, and carrying two cannon, it could climb to 6000m (19,685ft) in only a little more than 6 minutes 30 seconds. Although Göring had expected 1000 He 162s

Above: *Powered by two DB 603 engines, one in the nose and one in the rear fuselage, the Dornier Do 335A Pfeil was capable of 763km/h (474mph) but never flew operationally.*

to be built each month in factories at ground level and in salt and potassium mines by the spring of 1945, only 250-300 were actually completed with just 116 entering Luftwaffe service. Few were encountered by Allied pilots.

Messerschmitt was far more successful in its efforts to get its reaction-motor warplanes into service. Its Me 163 Komet became the first ever rocket-powered interceptor to be deployed operationally and its Me 262 became the first German turbojet-powered fighter. The Komet was a stubby, tailless single-seater powered by a Walter 109-509A-2 motor fueled by liquid propellants known as T-Stoff (hydrogen peroxide and water) and C-Stoff (hydrazine hydrate, methyl alcohol and water). The thrust of 1700kg (3748lbs) allowed a maximum level speed of 960km/h (597mph), though endurance was only a few minutes. The Me 163 was first flown as a prototype on full power at Peenemünde on 13 August 1941.

Armed with two cannon, the production Me 163B-1 Komet equipped Jagdgeschwader 400, its three Staffeln gathering at Brandis in July 1944. The first interceptions were made on 16 August that year, but none of the USAAF Flying Fortress bombers were shot down. Some 300 Komets were completed but the type claimed only nine Allied aircraft destroyed.

Because of delayed delivery of Junkers Jumo 004A turbojet engines to Messerschmitt, a prototype Me 262 jet fighter did not fly on turbojet power alone until 18 July 1942. A number of preproduction Me 262s were delivered to the evaluation unit Erprobungskommando 262 from April 1944, based at Lechfeld, which subsequently took the initial full-production Me 262A-1a single-seat four-cannon fighters. A fine aircraft with clean lines, capable of 868km/h (539mph) on the power of two underwing 900kg (1984lb) static thrust 004Bs, the Schwalbe fighter had barely begun leaving production lines when Hitler ordered its substitution by the Me 262A-2a Sturmvogel fighter-bomber because of its provision for two 250kg bombs or one weighing 500kg. By November 1944, however, the situation was so desperate for Germany that the fighter variant was reinstated.

Production of the Me 262 totalled only 1433 examples, way below the scheduled number, of which only some 200 became operational. About half those in service were

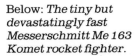
Below: *The tiny but devastatingly fast Messerschmitt Me 163 Komet rocket fighter.*

Above: *An abandoned Messerschmitt Me 262, as found by the advancing Allies.*

Left: *A captured Arado Ar 234B-1/b Blitz taken to the US for study by the Air Technical Service Command.*

lost during operations, but they claimed many Allied aircraft. At least 11 Luftwaffe Me 262 pilots became 'aces' (with five or more air victories), with Oberstleutnant Heinz Bär of JV 44 claiming 16 Allied aircraft. Eight of the other 10 pilots were from JG 7, who between them managed at least 75 kills. JG 7 overall was responsible for well over 400 Allied aircraft destroyed. Of these, three-quarters were four-engined heavy bombers, with many lost to salvoes of R4M unguided rockets fired from Me 262A-1bs. This period marked the first widespread use of air-to-air rockets and these proved particularly devastating against the large daylight formations of USAAF B-17s and B-24s. Other versions of the Me 262 built included the tandem two-seat Me 262B-1a/U1 and B-2a night fighters.

While the Me 262 was undoubtedly Germany's most important jet aircraft of the war, the very last Luftwaffe sortie over Britain was conducted on 10 April 1945 by an Arado Ar 234B Blitz reconnaissance jet of

KG 76 – incidentally the same day the USAAF lost 19 bombers and eight escort fighters to Me 262s during a raid on targets near Berlin. Although well used as a reconnaissance aircraft, indeed first operated in Ar 234A reconnaissance form from Juvincourt on 20 July 1944, the Blitz is best remembered as the only turbojet bomber of the war.

First flown as a prototype on 15 June 1943 after long delays in obtaining the two Junkers Jumo 004A turbojets, the single-seat Ar 234 went through a period of development which led to the adoption of a conventional retractable undercarriage instead of the original jettisonable take-off trolley and landing skids. The Ar 234 had also been designed to use a pressurized cockpit for the pilot, who was to sit on an ejection seat.

Following production of reconnaissance aircraft, the Ar 234B-2 began to appear. This was suited to both reconnaissance and bombing roles and possessed a maximum speed of 742km/h (461mph) on the power of two 900kg (1984lbs) static thrust Jumo 004B

tinued for a month. During March 1945 Ar 234s and Me 262s attempted to hold up the Allied crossings of the Rhine and proved capable of very high speed and accurate attacks, but fuel shortages thereafter greatly reduced Ar 234 operations. Fewer than 250 production Blitz bombers had been completed by the end of the war. Junkers, too, produced jet bombers, but only in prototype form as four-engined aircraft with forward-swept wings.

The only Allied turbojet-powered warplane to become operational in a combat role was Britain's Gloster Meteor fighter, the US Bell P-59 Airacomet being used mainly as a jet fighter trainer though capable of 665km/h (413mph) on the power of two General Electric J31 engines. Gloster had been given the contract to produce the airframes for a new type of fighter after it had constructed the E.28/39, Britain's first experimental jet aircraft that had taken to the air on the power of a Frank Whittle/Power Jets engine on 15 May 1941.

Unlike the Messerschmitt Me 262, the Meteor was designed to carry its engines within the wing; the first prototype to fly took to the air on 5 March 1943. Various turbojet engines were flown in the F.9/40 prototypes, but the initial production single-seat Gloster Meteor F.Mk 1 four-cannon fighter used two 771kg (1700lb) static thrust

Above: *Two of 13 service-evaluation examples of the Bell YP-59A Airacomet.*

Below: *A Lockheed XP-80A, powered by a General Electric J33 (I-40) turbojet and first flown in 1944.*

turbojets. Capable of using RATOG (rocket assisted take-off gear) and armed with two rearward-firing cannon and various warloads including one 1000kg and two 500kg bombs, the first B-2s became available to KG 76 in October 1944. The first bomber missions were pinpoint attacks on Allied targets during the Ardennes offensive, which started on 16 December 1944 and con-

Rolls-Royce Welland I turbojets developed from the original Whittle/Power Jets engines. Capable of 676km/h (420mph), Meteor F.Mk 1s went to No 616 Squadron from 12 July 1944 and were declared operational on the 27th, flying anti-V-1 sorties on that day. Only 20 F.Mk 1s were completed, followed by 793km/h (495mph) F.Mk 3s, most of the 280 built flying on two 907kg (2000lb) static thrust Rolls-Royce Derwent I engines. The mark had provision to carry a fuselage drop-tank to increase range.

In 1945 Meteor F.Mk 3s became active with the 2nd Tactical Air Force, operating first from a base close to Brussels. As far as is known, no Meteor ever met an Me 262 or He 162 in air combat: the world had to wait for the Korean War of the 1950s for the first all-jet combats. Meteor production continued after the end of the war, while other Allied jet fighters that had appeared as prototypes in wartime (the British de Havilland Vampire and US Lockheed P-80 Shooting Star) went into service in peacetime. Interestingly, the Me 262 got a brief second life after the war as the S-92, built in Czechoslovakia.

The war in Europe had been hard fought over many years, with Britain standing almost alone at the beginning but later aided in its offensive against Germany by armadas of American bombers. Meanwhile, other fronts had opened by the actions of the Italians and Japanese, and by the German invasion of the Soviet Union.

Below: Gloster Meteor 1s at Farnborough in June 1944, about to take off for Manston to equip the RAF's No 616 Squadron.

CHAPTER 4

AFRICAN AIR WAR

On 10 June 1940 Italy joined the fray by declaring war on the Allies, followed by an immediate invasion of Southern France. This was just days before France capitulated and was an action that country was not to forget quickly. For a little more than three years Italy asserted itself over a wide area in and around the Aegean and Mediterranean, in the Balkans and North Africa and the Middle East, and was heavily committed to the invasion of Greece. Its air force raided Britain, and Italian forces fought on the Eastern Front against the Soviet Union.

Under Benito Mussolini's guidance, the Regia Aeronautica (Italian air force) had grown steadily in size and competence over many years, retaining its tradition begun during World War I of a strong multi-engined strategic bomber force. Italy had shown itself to be both belligerent and militarily capable well before 1940, showing its might for the first time in October 1935 when Italian forces invaded Abyssinia (now Ethiopia) following nearly a year-long dispute over an area of the Somaliland border. In the fighting against poorly-armed tribesmen, Italy made widespread use of air power and this included air-dropping poison gas. Similarly, Italy took on a very substantial role on behalf of the Nationalists during the Spanish Civil War, for much of the time eclipsing even the German effort.

Italy's entry into World War II meant more to Britain than just the formation of the Axis alliance with Germany. Britain had used Italy as a staging point on its Empire air routes to Australia, Africa, the Middle East and India, and the air links to the Empire were now severed temporarily. On 11 June, the day after Italy's declaration of war, the Regia Aeronautica began its attacks on Malta, the British dependency strategically positioned close to the bottleneck between Sicily and Tunisia in the Mediterranean. These early attacks continued for well over two weeks. The only aircraft then available to defend Malta were four crated Gloster Sea Gladiators, which were hurriedly assembled. Three of these, named *Hope*, *Faith* and *Charity*, carved a legend for themselves by their truly epic defense of the island against seemingly overwhelming numbers, fighting alone until relieved by Hawker Hurricanes of No 261 Squadron that arrived on board the

Right: *A lone Messerschmitt Bf 110D-3 of KG 26 (foreground) offers protection for a large number of Junkers Ju 52/3m transports in North Africa.*

Above: *The Fairey Fulmar II two-seat carrier-borne naval fighter carried eight forward-firing (and sometimes one rear-mounted) machine guns. The Fulmar was widely used to defend convoys to Malta and the Soviet Union and saw action during Operation* Torch.

Below: *The ultimate development of the open-cockpit biplane fighter in Italy was the Fiat CR 42 Falco, which remained in use throughout Italy's involvement in the war.*

aircraft carrier HMS *Argus* on 2 August. Eventually (on 15 April 1942) the island of Malta was awarded the George Cross in recognition of its fortitude against these and later enemy actions. Britain was revenged for the attack on Malta on the night of 11-12 June 1940 when RAF Whitley bombers raided Genoa and Turin.

On 11 November 1940, the Regia Aeronautica carried out its only major air raid on Britain, but lack of suitable fighters to escort Italian bombers led to serious losses at the hands of the RAF. Then 13 months later, on 11 December 1941, Italy and Germany declared war on the United States, but it was not until 4 December 1942 that the USAAF used B-24 Liberators of the Ninth Army Air Force to mount an American attack on Italy, on this occasion raiding Naples.

In January 1943 Churchill and Roosevelt decided to strike at occupied Europe through the 'soft underbelly', with Sicily as the first invasion point. Just one of many attacks on Axis airfields in Sicily was that of 25 June, which saw 130 Flying Fortress bombers drop more than 300 tons of bombs on Messina.

Having also attacked Sardinia and Italy itself over a number of weeks, British and US armies invaded Sicily on 9 July and, by 8 September, an armistice meant that Italy's war against the Allies was over. However, Germany was not prepared to watch its former Axis partner change sides; on the following day German forces invaded Italy, while the Luftwaffe attacked Italian naval vessels *en route* to surrender to the Allies. It took many months of fierce fighting thereafter for the Allies to drive the invaders back, with Italy itself declaring war on Germany on 13 October 1943. On 22 January 1944 the Allies made large-scale landings at Anzio, supported by massive air cover; in the ensuing battle to keep the beach-head, substantial air attacks were made against German formations. By 11 May the Mediterranean Allied Air Forces had dropped about 26,000 tons of bombs on German lines of communication in Italy under Operation *Strangle*, and in August the same force was used to begin the liberation of Southern France.

European fighting aside, some of the hardest-fought battles against Italian forces were those in Africa and the Middle East where British, South African and other Allied forces (later also American) faced very substantial Italian strength and, later, Rommel's Afrika Korps. The war in this region had begun with small numbers of RAF Gladiator biplane fighters, Vickers Wellesley general-purpose bombers, Blenheim bombers, Vickers Vincent general-purpose biplanes and other outdated aircraft facing substantial numbers of Italian warplanes, both outdated and modern, which included Fiat CR 42 biplane fighters, IMAM Ro 37 close-support biplanes and Savoia-Marchetti trimotor bombers of the SM 79 Sparviero and SM 81 Pipistrello types. Interestingly, Royal Air Force Wellesleys were in action on the first day of the East African Campaign.

Above: *A camera is taken to a waiting Messerschmitt Bf 110 before a reconnaissance mission.*

Left: *A Savoia-Marchetti SM 79 Sparviero medium bomber displays its distinctive 'humped' fuselage. Note particularly the dorsal, ventral and beam gun positions.*

Both sides modernized as the fighting spread, with the Western Desert Air Force (comprising RAF, Australian and South African squadrons) receiving several American types among new warplanes. In August 1942 the US Twelfth Army Air Force was activated in the US for the expected invasion of North Africa, with air cover for the actual invasion in November (under Operation *Torch*) provided in part by the USAAF flying warplanes from US Navy aircraft carriers. In response to the invasion, however, the Luftwaffe strength in Tunis was quickly increased.

On 17 February 1943 the Mediterranean Air Command was established to take over from the Middle East Air Command, Northwest Africa Air Forces and Malta Air Command, allowing greater co-ordination of efforts in the region by the Allies. Over the next months the Allies gradually bottle-necked Italian and German forces into northern Tunisia, Axis aircraft making every effort to save the situation by carrying supplies from Sicily. To counter this the Allies began Operation *Flax* on 5 April 1943, making air attacks on transports shuttling between Sicily and Tunisia. These patrols

and attacks were highly successful, not only in disrupting supplies but stopping any evacuation that could ultimately strengthen Axis forces in Europe.

On 13 May the Axis forces in North Africa capitulated and the African campaign was at an end. The necessity for early Allied raids on Italian positions in Libya, the battles at the Egyptian border, the loss of Greece to German and Italian forces in April 1941 and the loss of Crete in May to a massive airborne assault under Germany's Operation *Mercury* – all this had forced the Allies to deploy many of its most modern aircraft to this region instead of using it as a refuge for outdated warplanes for which there were no immediate replacements. Similarly, Italy's biplanes slowly gave way to superior monoplane replacements, while Luftwaffe Bf 109s, Bf 110s and Ju 87s were subsequently joined by medium bombers and newer fighters.

Italy's only major air raid on the British Isles has been mounted by Fiat BR 20 Cicogna bombers, 440km/h (273mph) low-wing monoplanes powered by two 1000hp Fiat A.80 RC41 engines. Armed with four machine guns for defense and with a warload of 1600kg (3527lbs), 75 such aircraft had been grouped in Belgium for this offensive. Operating from October until recalled in January 1941, the bombers managed only night raids in small numbers after the 11 November attack, causing little trouble to the RAF. BR 20s were subsequently used during the invasion of Greece and assisted the Luftwaffe on the Eastern Front.

Of the many other aircraft operated by Italy, the two most important medium bombers were the Savoia-Marchetti SM 79

Above left: *Messerschmitt Bf 109s, possibly E-7/U2 sub-variants serving with 10 Staffel/JG 27, support the Afrika Korps around 1941.*

Above: *An Advanced Servicing Unit in Libya dismantles a crashed RAF Spitfire of No 145 Squadron, 1942. Both sides employed modern combat types in Africa.*

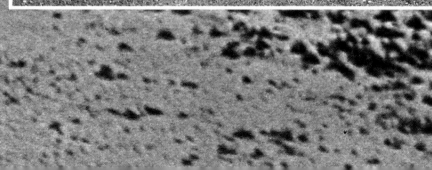

Top: *The flight deck of the US Navy escort carrier USS Santee pictured during Operation Torch off the North African coast.*

Above: *Wrecked RAF Blenheim bombers are seen in Greece in 1941 after that country fell to German forces.*

better of the two bombers. Apart from obvious configurational differences, the Alcione was mainly of wooden construction, whereas the Sparviero was mainly metal.

Italy deployed several other types of bomber and attack aircraft during the war, but only one type of heavy bomber — the 420km/h (261mph) Piaggio P.108B, powered by four 1500hp Piaggio P.XII RC 35 engines. Its debut came in 1942 in operations over Gibraltar, that British island of major strategic importance, flying with the 274th Squadriglia Bombardieri a Grande Raggio. Like all Italian bombers, it retained an overwater anti-shipping capability. In as much as the P.108B was its only four-engined bomber of the war, Italy was as neglectful of the heavy strategic bomber as Germany.

Other Italian bombers included the CRDA Cant Z.506B Airone twin-float seaplane, a type also ordered before the war by Poland and capable of 364km/h (226mph) on the power of three 750hp Alfa Romeo 126 RC 34 radial engines. It carried up to 1200kg (2646lbs) of bombs or torpedos. A twin Fiat A.74 RC 38-engined maritime bomber was the 390km/h (242mph) Fiat RS 14 floatplane. The very refined 530km/h (329mph) CRDA Cant Z.1018 Leone (two 1500hp Piaggio P.XII RC 35 engines and a warload of six 250kg bombs) had only just begun to enter service when Italy surrendered to the Allies. Other types included the Caproni bombers in the Ca 309 to Ca 314 series (also used by Norway as the Ca 310, among others) and the

Sparviero and the CRDA Cant Z.1007bis Alcione, both usually powered by three 1000hp Piaggio P.XI RC 40 engines. Both could undertake conventional bombing or torpedo-attack roles; their speeds were similar at 430km/h (267mph) and 455km/h (283mph) respectively, and almost identical range. Each of these aircraft was armed defensively with four machine guns.

The main difference between them came in the bombloads carried, with the Alcione carrying up to 2000kg (4409lbs) and the Sparviero 1200kg (2646lbs), although most historians accept that the latter was the trimotor Savoia-Marchetti SM 81 and SM 84. Another Savoia-Marchetti type was the twin-engined but little used SM 85. The SM 81 managed a speed and bombload of 340km/h (211mph) and 1000kg (2205lbs) respectively on the power of three 700hp Piaggio P.X engines.

Italian fighters ranged from open-cockpit biplanes and monoplanes to modern mono-planes of world class. Italy's involvement in the Spanish Civil War had brought the Fiat CR 32 biplane to the forefront of European attention, possessing all the attributes of a good fighter – speed, good armament and excellent maneuverability. Having been served so well by biplanes, Fiat was not anxious to follow the world trend for canti-lever monoplanes with retractable under-carriages without one further biplane and so, as a CR 32 replacement (the CR 32 itself remaining in service long enough to see

action in Africa and Greece), it produced the CR 42 Falco.

Incredibly for such an antiquated-looking fighter, the prototype did not make its first flight until 1939, but it was not only accepted for the Regia Aeronautica but also received export orders, including one for 34 from Belgium. With sesquiplane wings, a trousered and spatted fixed undercarriage, open cockpit for the pilot and initially just two guns (later increased to four), the CR 42 was capable of 450km/h (280mph) on the power of an 840hp Fiat A.74 RC 38 radial engine. CR 42s were employed as day and night fighters, bomber escorts and fighter-bombers, in the latter role proving particu-larly well suited to the deserts of North Africa where initial opposition was not too stiff (carrying perhaps two 100kg bombs). Production ended in 1943 after 1784 had been built, by which time more suitable types

Left: *The CRDA Cant Z.1007 bis Alcione was a trimotor medium bomber of wooden construction.*

Below: *Twin-finned Fiat BR 20 Cicogna bombers, many of which were lost in action over Britain, Greece and the Eastern Front.*

had been replacing CR 42s as fighters.

When Italy went to war in 1940, Fiat CR 32 and CR 42 open-cockpit biplanes comprised the bulk of the Regia Aeronautica's single-seat fighter strength. Though Fiat had mass produced the CR 42 to make it the most widely used fighter at that time, it had also constructed examples of its first cantilever low-wing monoplane fighter with a retractable undercarriage as the G 50 Freccia, although production had been slow since the first flight of a prototype in 1937. Fitted with the same engine as the CR 42 and carrying only two guns, the cleaner lines of the heavier G 50 allowed a top speed of 427km/h (293mph). Flown with open cockpits as a concession to Italian pilots, G 50s operated in most areas.

Fiat's finest achievement of the war in the field of single-seat fighters was undoubtedly the G 55 Centauro. Developed from an experimental version of the G 50, the G 55 attained a much cleaner aerodynamic form and greater performance by substituting a 1250hp Daimler-Benz DB 605A inline engine for the radial engine of its predecessor. This power plant allowed a less bulky fuselage. The pilot was given a fully enclosed cockpit and armament was raised to five guns. Capable of 620km/h (385mph), the G 55 was a world-class fighter, but none had reached operational status by the time of Italy's surrender to the Allies.

Fiat's A.74 radial engine was selected by other manufacturers for their own monoplane fighter designs, with the result that several early Italian fighters of this type were

both underpowered and bulky. One of the least successful in terms of orders was the Caproni-Vizzola F 5, another two-gun machine but managing a very respectable 510km/h (317mph). As the F 5 offered few advantages over some fighters already in production by 1940, only the small pre-production batch was completed and these were used as temporary night fighters from bases near Rome.

Among the best Italian fighters of the war were those designed by Macchi. The company's A.74-powered C 200 Saetta first flew as a prototype on 24 December 1937, and by the time Italy entered the war more than 150 production examples were in service. Still carrying only two guns, later supplemented by bombs when flown as a fighter-bomber, the Saetta was used on every front involving Italian forces. Production of warplanes by Italy was surprisingly low during World War II and it is interesting to note that C 200 production easily outstripped that of the Fiat G 50, even though only some 1000 C 200s had been completed by the end of the war. Maximum speed was 503km/h (313mph).

Like Fiat, Macchi found that the substitution of a German Daimler-Benz inline engine into its fighter paid dividends in performance terms. For Macchi, the resulting new fighter was the C 202 Folgore, which began to enter squadrons of the Regia Aeronautica in mid 1941. On the power of a 1075hp DB 601 or, later, its Alfa Romeo-built equivalent, the RA.1000 RC 41-I, the C 202 attained 600km/h (373mph). Progressively armed with two machine guns, four machine engine. The resulting new fighter became the C 205V Veltro, production examples using license-built Fiat RA.1050 RC 58 engines. Either armed with four machine guns or two machine guns and two cannon, the C 205 first entered service in 1943 as an interceptor to counter Allied activity over Sicily. But even its 642km/h (399mph) top speed could not save the situation, as fewer than 70 had reached squadron service before the Italian capitulation.

The other important manufacturer of fighters in Italy during World War II was Reggiane, a company with links stretching back to World War I when it constructed Caproni aircraft under contract. Resuming aircraft manufacture in 1937, as part of the Caproni group, its first fighter was the Re 2000 Falco I, a single-seater with a semi-elliptical monoplane wing and featuring a long cockpit canopy. Powered by a 986hp Piaggio P.XI RC 40 radial, twin-gunned and possessing a speed of 530km/h (329mph), it proved capable of outflying the Macchi C 200 but was structurally weaker and so was only used in very small numbers by the Italian Navy from September 1942 and exported.

Reggiane also saw the benefits accruing from the DB 601A engine and produced a revised fighter as the Re 2001 Falco II in 1940. In production form, the Re 2001 used the Italian-built version of the engine, which

Above: *The Piaggio P.108B was Italy's only four-engined heavy bomber of the war.*

Right: *The Macchi C 200 Saetta was typical of Italy's early monoplane fighters in that it had to fly on a low-powered radial engine. Most C 200s were operated with an open cockpit, unlike the pictured example.*

guns and then two guns and two cannon, about 1500 were completed before the Italian capitulation in 1943; these served in Libya, on the Eastern Front and as escorts for bombers raiding Malta.

Though excellent in many respects, the C 202 was still not as capable as the latest Allied fighters and many undertook fighter-bomber sorties. Macchi produced the performance required, however, boosting power to 1250hp by the use of a DB 605A

gave it a maximum speed of 545km/h (339mph). Going through similar armament updates to the Macchi C 202, it made its first sortie in May 1942 in operations against Malta and thereafter was used in North Africa, Sicily and as a night fighter in Italy. Production amounted to only 252 machines.

Reggiane's next combat aircraft looked more like the Re 2000 than the later Re 2001, having a 1125hp Piaggio P.XIX RC 35 radial engine installed but designed specifically as a fighter-bomber. With a maximum speed of 538km/h (334mph) but also possessing an important increase in range and capable of carrying 650kg (1433lbs) of bombs, the Re 2002 Ariete was a useful warplane. However, it entered service too late to be of much help, around 40 aircraft going to two squadrons. Nevertheless, the Ariete saw action against the Allied landings in Sicily.

Reggiane's RA 1050 RC 58-engined fighter, the Re 2005 Sagittario, also came on the scene too late to change the course of Italy's fate, with fewer than 50 available in the closing stages of Italy's war against the Allies. Highly maneuverable, as were all Reggiane fighters, with a top speed of 629mph (391mph), Re 2005s were armed with two machine guns and three cannon and were based in Sicily, Naples and elsewhere during the Allied advance. After the Armistice some Re 2005s, in company with other Italian warplanes, fought on with the pro-German Aviazione della RSI, serving in Rumania and Germany.

Italy had little success in its quest for a twin-engined fighter and fighter-bomber,

the three-seat Fiat CR 25 that first entered service in Sicily in 1941 proving underpowered on A.74 RC 38 engines and being transferred to maritime reconnaissance and then transport duties. Maxium speed was 490km/h (304mph). Similarly, the much more businesslike single-seat IMAM Ro 57, also using A.74 RC 38 engines and capable of 500km/h (311mph), was viewed as underpowered and lacking maneuverability and was used from 1942 mainly as an attack aircraft and dive bomber, armed with two machine guns (sometimes also two cannon) plus 500kg (1102lbs) of bombs.

In addition to indigenous aircraft, the Regia Aeronautica flew various foreign warplanes, including French Dewoitine D 520 fighters and LeO 451 bombers. The best remembered of these, however, were German-built aircraft such as the Ju 87, Bf 109, Bf 110 and Do 217J.

Despite its early strength of numbers and, later, the arrival of the German Afrika Korps, Italy had been vanquished by the co-ordinated actions of Commonwealth nations, assisted subsequently by the Americans. In

Bottom: *The RAF Kittyhawk IA was equivalent to the USAAF's P-40E Warhawk.*

this region, as in others, the Allies had managed to live through the most difficult days, the heat and the sand, building gradually upon their few early successes and eventually gaining air supremacy. By deploying in the region aircraft like the Tomahawk, Kittyhawk, Maryland, B-25 Mitchell, Spitfire and Hurricane, the Allies had outclassed the enemy in the air, having also had to fight the Vichy French as British and American forces landed in Algeria and Morocco in late 1942 to push Rommel east.

Italy's top fighter 'ace' of the war had been Maj Adriano Visconti, who gained 26 confirmed victories. This figure should be viewed in the context that Britain's top ace of the war, Gp Capt J.E. Johnson, gained only 38 victories, the USAAF's Maj Richard I. Bong gained 40 and the top aces from Australia, Belgium, Canada, Czechoslovakia, Denmark, France, Hungary, Ireland, the Netherlands, New Zealand, Norway, Poland and South Africa each gained between five and 43 victories. The aces that built up huge totals, excluding Finland's F/Mstr Juutualainen with 94, Japan's Sub Officer Nishizawa with 103, Rumania's Capt Prince Constantine Cantacuzino with 60 and Russia's Guards Col Kozhedub with 62, were exclusively Austrian and German, with the former's Maj Walter Nowotny gaining 258 and the top German ace, Maj Erich Hartmann, gaining no fewer than 352 victories. Indeed, 35 German pilots gained over 150 victories each. A high proportion of these colossal totals, and all of Hartmann's 352, were won on the Eastern Front, where the well-equipped and prepared Luftwaffe faced a large Soviet air force flying mostly outdated aircraft. This onslaught began with Operation *Barbarossa*.

Below: *A Spitfire VB of No 417 Squadron, RCAF, based in Italy and pictured in 1944.*

CHAPTER 5

OPERATION BARBAROSSA

Throughout the 1930s the Soviet Union made tremendous progress in aircraft design and manufacturing capability, studying air warfare tactics and planning for the VVS (air force) and AVMF (naval air force) to have the best equipment. Because of its turbulent past the whole vast country was geared to war, and the number of men in uniform exceeded that in any other part of the world. To attack the Soviet Union might have seemed an act of lunacy.

Yet the German Chancellor, Adolf Hitler, planned to do just this. He was not obliged to attack the Russians, and in fact had sewn up a detailed treaty with them immediately before launching World War II. His motives were based upon deep dislike and mistrust, on a wish to avoid what he saw as a threat from the East, and on the urgent need for oil for his mighty war machine. He planned that his armies should scythe forwards in vast pincer movements, each pincer gathering in 100,000 to 200,000 men and their equipment, so that a single German army should swallow up a whole succession of inferior Soviet armies. After he had invaded Moscow and the Caucasian oilfields his armies would stop and set up a frontier against the few demoralized and scattered peasants who might be left in Siberia.

His poor assessment of Soviet fighting capability rested in large degree on the air war in Spain in 1936-39. Here the latest Soviet fighters, the Polikarpov I-15 and I-16, had done well until the Nationalists had received early Bf 109Es; then the Soviet-built fighters had been routed. Of course, it was appreciated that they were not exactly new designs; Polikarpov had created them in 1933 as a matched pair because the VVS staff could not decide whether to go for the speedy monoplane or the agile biplane and decided to use both in partnership (a decision similar to that made in Italy).

First flown in October 1933, the I-15 was the biplane, with a fuselage made from welded steel tubes and mainly wooden wings, with fabric covering almost everywhere. With a gross weight of 1681kg (3706lbs), when powered by the latest 710hp M-25 (Cyclone) engine it possessed a top speed of 365km/h (227mph) and armament was two machine guns. It had been followed by the I-152 or I-15*bis*, with four guns and slightly

Left: *Rear gunner at the ready, a Luftwaffe Junkers Ju 88 prepares for a bombing mission. The type served in every theater in which the Germans fought.*

better performance with a 750hp engine. The latest of the biplanes was the I-153, with a 1000hp M-62 engine and retractable undercarriage, and also the ability to carry a fair load of bombs or rockets. The I-153 had fought Japanese monoplanes in Outer Mongolia from May 1939, but was regarded as obsolescent by the Luftwaffe.

As for the I-16, this had been the world's most advanced fighter when it first flew on 31 December 1933, because, despite its rather dated structure with a wooden fuselage and fabric-covered wing, it had a retractable undercarriage, unbraced cantilever monoplane wing, well-cowled engine driving a variable-pitch propeller and an enclosed cockpit. Intelligence showed, however, that it was tricky to fly and, despite being updated with the same 950/1000hp engine as the I-153 and given heavier armament such as four fast-firing machine guns or two 20mm cannon, it was much slower than the Bf 109E at 464-489km/h (288-304mph) and far inferior in many other significant respects.

There was, however, one Soviet type that did perform impressively in Spain; this was the Tupolev SB-2 medium bomber. First flown in April 1934, this was a very clean monoplane of all-metal stressed-skin construction, typically carrying six 100kg bombs and with a maximum speed of 450km/h (280mph) in SB-2bis form with 960hp M-103 engines. Most had three or four machine guns for defense, late versions having a dorsal turret, but again its impressive performance against old biplane fighters was not considered to reflect the situation against the Bf 109.

All these adverse assessments were confirmed during the Soviet Union's 'Winter War' against plucky Finland in 1939-40, when the Soviets were almost universally condemned for trying to overwhelm a weak neighbor. The giant Tupolev TB-3 heavy bomber, first flown in 1930, was used to mount attacks on Finnish cities, but again was considered to have no chance against modern defenses. Also used in the Winter War was the Ilyushin DB-3B, DB-3M and later Il-4, all long-range bombers similar to the B-18 or early Wellington. With two engines in the 800/1100hp class, they were able to carry about 1000kg (2205lbs) of bombs or a torpedo, but again appeared easy prey for the Bf 109 or German flak.

Though German intelligence certainly did not fall for the popular Western belief that, like the Japanese, all the Soviets could do was make inferior copies of old Western aircraft, the general opinion was that the Luftwaffe would have little trouble gaining mastery of the air. The assessment proved correct, and Hitler's prediction that the main campaign would be over in six to eight weeks at first looked like being realized. The casualties suffered in men and matériel by the Soviet forces in the first month from the launch of Operation Barbarossa in the small hours of 22 June 1941 exceeded anything seen in previous history. Despite repeated and obvious indications and warnings, the attack caught the Soviet forces totally off-guard. Aircraft were parked in neat rows on front-line airfields, and nearly 1500 of 1811 Soviet aircraft destroyed for the loss of 35 Luftwaffe machines in the first day were caught on the ground. Within a week, more than half the

Above: *A Polikarpov I-15bis, presumably captured by the Finnish air force during the course of the Winter War.*

Right: *Once the world's most advanced fighter, the Polikarpov I-16 was outdated by 1941.*

Soviet front-line strength had been destroyed or captured, and the proportion rose to three-quarters after 30 days. By September, urgent plans were being made to abandon most of the factories and try to evacuate men and tools much further to the east.

It so happened that Hitler attacked at the worst possible moment for the Soviets. Thousands of old aircraft were in front-line service but were largely ineffectual in attack and, in any case, were destroyed in droves. The newer types, most of which were known to the Germans, had just begun to get into service in numbers. Compared to the previous generation they were much more powerful, faster and needed a different style of piloting. With much greater weights and smaller wings they landed at speeds typically 50 per cent faster than before, and this posed great problems on the rough grass fields and board airstrips of the Soviet airbases. It was even harder when these bases were overrun and the challenging new fighters and bombers had to operate from makeshift fields. Casualties were terrible, and even in the air the new machines were often difficult to fly. There was even a joke that the Lavochkin LaGG-3, a fast and rugged fighter made of wood, got its designation from the description *Lakirovannii Garantirovannii Grob*, meaning guaranteed varnished coffin! Even the new types did not seem able to make much impression on the Luftwaffe.

The LaGG was the first product of a new group of designers, Lavochkin, Gorbunov and Gudkov, who teamed up in September 1938 to design a fighter skinned with special multi-ply wood laminations impregnated with adhesive. As with most of the new Soviet fighters, they went for high performance,

Above: *Luftwaffe Junkers Ju 87D-1s of Gruppen Stab II/StG 2 operated on the Eastern Front against Soviet forces in 1942.*

Left: *Although Dornier Do 17Zs operated on the Eastern Front until November 1942, they were flown after 1941 only in very small numbers in the hands of volunteers from the Croatian air force.*

combining a big 1050hp M-105P engine with a small airframe (the wing area, for example, being 188.5 sq ft, compared with 242 sq ft for a Spitfire). Again like the other new fighters, this made maneuverability difficult and it was almost impossible to carry heavy armament. Most LaGG fighters had a single cannon and two machine guns, yet their maximum speed of some 575km/h (357mph) was little higher than that of a Bf 109E and well below the speed of later Messerschmitts.

Perhaps even less successful was the first MiG, created by the equally new partnership of Mikoyan and Gurevich. First flown in April 1940, the MiG-1 was again a conventional type of fighter, with almost exactly the same small size of wing as the LaGG but with a monster engine: the 1350hp AM-35A, much bigger even than the British Griffon. The MiG could hardly avoid being fast, but attempts were made to cure some of the worst faults with the 640km/h (398mph) MiG-3,

Opposite: *On the night of 21-22 July 1941, Luftwaffe Dorniers carried out the first night attack on Moscow.*

Above: *A Ilyushin Il-2 two-seater exhibited in Poland. To Stalin's Army, it was considered as important as 'air and bread.'*

Right: *Ilyushin Il-4 (originally known as DB-3F) bombers, initially all-metal aircraft but redesigned to use some wooden components following shortages of alloys.*

which soon replaced the Dash-1 in production. Even so, it was just as tricky to fly, undergunned (with one heavy machine gun and two rifle-caliber weapons) and certainly no match for its enemies, many of which were flown by pilots who had been constantly in combat since Spain and had become deadly opponents.

Best of the new Soviet fighters was probably the Yak-1, flown as the I-26 prototype on 1 January 1940. Yet again, this machine had the same size wing as the LaGG and was of mixed construction with a steel-tube fuselage and wooden wing. Powered by a 1050hp M-105P, it reached about 600km/h (373mph)

but again carried inadequate armament in one 20mm cannon and two machine guns. Nevertheless, on the rare occasions when it was flown by a skilled pilot it could usually get the better of a Messerschmitt unless the latter was in the hands of one of the great *experten*. Tremendous efforts were put into improving the Yaks, and the Yak-7A fighter which was produced in 1941 was simpler, tougher and generally better than the Yak-1.

On the bomber side, the lumbering TB-3 was soon consigned to transport roles well behind the Front, while the SB-2 and faster SB-3 bore the brunt of early tactical bombing despite colossal losses. The Ilyushin Il-4 was built in large numbers as the chief long-range bomber, though it was older DB-3s flown by Naval Aviation pilots which bombed Berlin on the night of 7-8 August 1941. The Front then moved too far to the east for Berlin to be reached, though Il-4s served on Northern and Black Sea Fronts as torpedo bombers. For longer ranges the Tupolev bureau, Petlyakov's brigade, had produced the big TB-7 four-engined heavy bomber, which in 1940 was redesignated Pe-8 in honour of its designer. Powered by 1350hp AM-35A engines, it was used in small numbers but accomplished little despite its range of 4700km (2920 miles) with 2000kg (4409lbs) of bombs. About 25 were available for the attack on Berlin on the night of 7-8 August 1941, but they had been refitted with troublesome ACh-30B diesel engines. Of 18 which actually flew from the runway, 11 reached Berlin and six got back.

The ACh-30B diesel was also fitted to examples of another long-range bomber, the Yermolayev Yer-2. Originally designated DB-240 and first flown in June 1940, this outstanding twin-engined machine was about as big as an Il-4 but almost twice as heavy and much more powerful. It had good defensive armament and armor, could carry 3000kg (6615lbs) of bombs internally and had good performance, though this varied greatly depending on the engines fitted. About 300 were built in a second series with the diesel engines, and these were slower than the M-105-engined examples at 446km/h (277mph) but had a range of the order of 5000km (3107 miles).

In 1941 there were still large numbers of obsolescent tactical biplanes such as the Kochyerigin DI-6, Polikarpov R-5 and Polikarpov R-Z. The R-10, designed as the KhAI-5 by Nyeman's brigade, was a slightly later monoplane used in the Winter War, but this too was outclassed. Just coming into use in numbers, Sukhoi's Su-2 (until 1941 called the BB-1) looked like a radial-engined Fairey Battle with a turret, and in fact its casualties were reminiscent of those suffered by the British light bomber. Powered by a 1000hp M-88B engine, the two-seat Su-2 could only reach about 375km/h (233mph) at sea level — and, though it could carry about 400kg (882lbs) of bombs internally as well as rockets under the wing, it was poorly defended with a single machine gun in the turret. The pilot had four more guns in the wing, but was hardly ever presented with a chance to use them.

At first glance, one might have thought casualties among the Il-2 regiments would have been just as severe. Ilyushin's attack machine was only fractionally faster than the Su-2 at sea level, a typical figure being 403km/h (250mph) and, being a single-seater, it had no rear defense at all. The big difference lay in the exceptional armor protection of the Ilyushin which, when it first flew in October 1940, had been designated BSh-2 (armored assault type 2). Powered by a 1665hp AM-38 liquid-cooled engine, the Il-2 was the latest of a series of Soviet attack machines in which the pilot and other important items were surrounded by a veritable bath of armor, weighing in this case 700kg (1543lbs). It took tremendous effort to get the armor into production, and its weight so

Below: *The Petlyakov Pe-2, a Soviet bomber that could outstrip its fighter escort.*

degraded performance that the BSh-2 went into production as a single-seater, even though it had been designed as a two-seater with a rear defensive gun; Ilyushin did not believe in the VVS argument that the Il-2 would be escorted by fighters which would protect it.

After 22 June 1941 the new Il-2s were shot down in droves, despite their armor, and there was an urgent rethink. This led to some machines being modified by the operating regiments' workshops to carry a rear gunner, while in early 1942 the single-seaters were replaced with the Il-2M, Il-2 Type 3 and 3M, all with a rear gunner firing a 12.7mm UBT heavy machine gun. This did much to

non and two machine guns firing ahead. It was a single-seater, with the pilot heavily protected by slabs of armor and special glass 75mm (3in) thick. The resulting machine seemed to have potential, but it was sluggish, underpowered and the pilot's view was extremely poor.

The Luftwaffe persisted in the new Henschel, however, because the same maker's little Hs 123A biplane had done extremely well in the close-support role from the Spanish Civil War onwards. First flown in May 1933, the Hs 123 was a small and nimble biplane with only two machine guns and a top speed at sea level of 333km/h (207mph) but able to carry four 50kg bombs

Right: The obsolescent Polikarpov Po-2 proved invaluable in harassing German troops.

deter the Luftwaffe fighters. From the start, the Il-2 had carried RS-82 and RS-132 heavy rockets which punched through the rear and side armor of even the Tiger tanks, as well as heavy forward-firing cannon (first the 20mm ShVAK, then the 23mm VYa and, in the Type 3 and 3M, the massive 37mm NS-OKB-16). Such weapons devastated the massed Panzers, and from quite early in the Eastern Front campaign the Il-2, popularly called the *Shturmovik*, played perhaps the greatest role of any single aircraft in stopping the invaders. Production lagged at first, until Stalin sent a telegram saying 'The Red Army needs the Il-2 like it needs air and bread.' Output then soared, and kept on climbing until 36,163 had been built, more than for any other single aircraft type in history.

The Luftwaffe had a direct counterpart to the Il-2 on the Eastern Front in the Henschel Hs 129. This had won a competition in 1939 for a close-support aircraft with two quite low-powered engines but heavy armor and forward-firing guns. The first version, the Hs 129A, had two 465hp Argus As 410A engines and carried two 20mm MG FF can-

or containers of small anti-personnel bombs. It was able to avoid much hostile fire because of its superb pilot view and in-flight agility. Hs 123s did well against low-powered biplane opposition encountered on the Eastern Front, and as their numbers dwindled many calls came for their production to be restarted once more.

By far the most important of the Hs 123A's biplane opponents was the Polikarpov Po-2 (until 1941 called the U-2), a trainer in the class of the Tiger Moth. Like all the Soviet aircraft, this was so tough and simple it just kept going in conditions so harsh or cold that more complex machines either developed faults or simply refused to start. Increasingly the Po-2s, puttering along at about 113km/h (70mph), were used to reconnoitre the front line, drop bombs, fire machine guns and rockets and harass the enemy even in the depths of the forests, especially by night. The German troops said 'The Po-2 looks over the window sills of the buildings to see if we're inside!' The Luftwaffe became so rattled by its inability to stop the Po-2s, even versions with propaganda loudspeakers broadcasting in

Above: The Yakovlev Yak-9P was the ultimate development of the Soviet piston-engined fighter, this version appearing at the end of the war.

Right: An example of the Soviet Lavochkin La-7, preserved in Prague.

German, that it brought in large numbers of former trainers such as the He 72, Ar 66 and Go 145 to equip numerous night harassment and close-support squadrons.

As for the Hs 129, this matured by 1942 into the slightly bigger Hs 129B with more cockpit windows, heavier armament and 700hp Gnome-Rhône 14M radial engines already in production in France. Even though the range of view actually worsened because of the bulkier engines, the Hs 129B went into action on the Eastern and Tunisian Fronts in late 1942. It could reach about 355km/h (220mph) at sea level, but later models with a big 30mm MK 103 gun slung underneath could not reach 290km/h (180mph) at sea level, and a few just struggled into the air with the BK 75mm anti-tank gun which could even stop a Josef Stalin III with one shot.

As the Germans had not planned on a long war there were no new types to replace the old bombers such as the He 111 and Do 17Z. The latter, powered by its 1000hp Fafnir engines, continued to soldier on into 1943

and even 1944 with the Finns. In contrast the Soviets did introduce improved types, and two of the very best were fast twin-engined attack bombers.

One that got into action right at the start of the campaign was the Petlyakov Pe-2, very like Britain's Mosquito but made of metal and with upper and lower rear gunners. Powered by two 1260hp VK-105PF engines, beautifully installed with radiators inside the wing (a trick also adopted by the Mosquito), the Pe-2 could carry a bombload of 1600kg (3527lbs) yet reach 450km/h (280mph) at sea level and 580km/h (360mph) at its best height. When RAF Hurricanes went to the aid of the Soviets in 1941 they were amazed to find that, even at full throttle, they could not keep up with the Pe-2 bombers they were detailed to escort.

Not so the Soviet fighters which, starting small and powerful, were progressively improved with refined airframes and better engines. The MiG team gave up, though it produced a succession of the war period's best ultra-high-altitude fighter prototypes.

Lavochkin pressed ahead without his partners and, toiling against terrible difficulties – out of doors in a Siberian winter – because he was out of favor with Stalin, he eventually managed to convert the unpopular LaGG-3 to take the ASh-82 radial engine.

This transformed the wooden fighter into one of the best combat aircraft on the Eastern Front, as the La-5, and this had just got into service by the Stalingrad débâcle in early 1943. Many hundreds were engaged in the Battle of Kursk in June 1943 and the 1700hp engine – by this time the direct-injection ASh-82FN variety – gave a speed of over 644km/h (400mph), usually with an armament of two 20mm ShVAK cannon above the fuselage. During 1942-44 some 9921 of these fighters were built, following 6528 liquid-cooled LaGGs, and the 1944 model was the improved La-7 which often added a third cannon and yet reached 680km/h (423mph).

Yak's fighters were made in even greater numbers. Following 8721 Yak-1s and about 5000 Yak-7 fighters (out of 6399 of all Yak-7 versions), the breed divided, the Yak-9

becoming the main long-range model and the hotted-up Yak-3 the dogfighter. The Yak-9 introduced a host of refinements, which by 1944 included a metal wing which left more room inside for fuel, so that the Yak-9DD had enough range to enable the Soviets to fly a whole regiment to Bari in southern Italy to support Communist partisans in the Balkans. By August 1945 total Yak-9 production in many sub-types had reached 16,769. The smaller and exceedingly agile Yak-3 had a very late start and did not get into production until July 1944, but by May 1945 this line had terminated at 4845 aircraft produced. Powered by the 1300hp VK-105PF-2, the Yak-3 typically had a loaded weight of only 2660kg (5864lbs) and, with armament of only one 20mm ShVAK and two BS or ShKAS machine guns, it out-turned all Luftwaffe fighters as well as reaching 660km/h (410mph).

Such performance was well beyond the capability of any of the Western fighters supplied to the Soviet Union, the most numerous being the Bell P-39 Airacobra

Above: *Bell P-39Q Airacobras in USAAF markings, photographed in 1945. By far the most important version, with more than 4900 built, a very large number of P-39Qs were transferred to the Soviet Union under Lend-Lease arrangements.*

Below: *Developed from the P-39, the P-63 Kingcobra was mainly produced for Soviet use, although a substantial number of both types also went to France. This civil-registered P-63 is representative of a French-flown fighter.*

and P-63 Kingcobra. Distinguished by their unique layout, with the 1300hp Allison V-1710 engine amidships at the center of gravity driving the propeller via a long shaft, and with tricycle-type undercarriage, the various P-39 versions could reach about 604km/h (375mph) and typically had armament of one heavy cannon with 30 shells and four or six machine guns. The Soviet Union received about 5000 of these fighters, which

proved more popular than they had in the West. The P-63, which followed the P-39 in October 1943, differed only in fairly minor ways, though it was actually a completely new design. Able to reach about 660km/h (410mph), the same as the Yak-3, it was not in other respects in the same class, the rate of climb, acceleration and maneuverability being pedestrian by comparison. Like the P-39, the pilot boarded the aircraft by opening a car-type door on either side. The P-63 versions were all quite tough and useful, and they did a good job on the Eastern Front in the tactical attack role, carrying fair armament of one cannon, four machine guns and

three 500lb bombs. A total of 3300 was built, of which no fewer than 2421 were shipped to the Soviet Union.

Chronologically the last important type to go into action on the Eastern Front was the Tupolev Tu-2. Designed by Tupolev and his team in 1937-40, the prototype ANT-58 flew on 29 January 1941. The objective had been stated vaguely as an 'aircraft to beat the Ju 88,' and the ANT-58 had 1400hp liquid-cooled AM-37 engines, big slatted dive brakes, twin fins and upper and lower rear guns like the Pe-2, though the Tupolev was appreciably bigger. It showed tremendous performance, reaching 635km/h (395mph) despite having an internal bay for 3000kg (6614lbs) of bombs. Development was subsequently rather protracted and time-consuming, but the production Tu-2 was eventually accepted in early 1943 and, following further last-minute modification, it began to reach front-line troops in spring 1944. It was received ecstatically, the big

bomber now carrying a maximum load of 4000kg (8818lbs) yet handling like a small fighter. Powered by two 1850hp ASh-82FN radials, it had slowed to about 547km/h (340mph) by this time, not only because production machines often weigh far more than prototypes, but because the Tu-2 was now burdened with a take-off weight of over 11,340kg (25,000lbs). From it stemmed possibly the most diverse series of offshoot aircraft of any World War II type, some being physically larger and having a bigger nose and a crew compartment for two pilots side-by-side.

The later Tu-2 developments emerged into a world of jets, and where current long-range bombers were dominated by the B-29. After failing to obtain any B-29s from the US, Stalin simply commandeered three which force-landed in Soviet territory and had them copied as the Tu-4. From this stemmed all the postwar Tupolev piston, turboprop and jet long-range bombers.

CHAPTER 6

ONE DAY IN DECEMBER

Just as Operation *Barbarossa* caught the Soviet Union totally unprepared despite several warnings, so the Japanese attack on Pearl Harbor, Hawaii, achieved absolute surprise despite clear indications, mounting tension, the ability to read Japanese codes and the prophecy of the great General 'Billy' Mitchell that war with Japan would start by an attack on Pearl Harbor 'on a quiet Sunday morning.' Sunday 7 December 1941 was quiet enough, and when a young operator on a hilltop saw a formation of unidentified aircraft on his newly-installed radar the answer he got from higher authority was that they must be B-17s arriving on an exercise from California.

They were not B-17s but the *Teishin Butai* (strike force) from six giant carriers: 135 Mitsubishi A6M2 fighters, 135 Aichi D3A1 dive bombers and 144 Nakajima B5N2 torpedo bombers. Going about their business in two giant waves, they devastated the US Pacific Fleet, as well as virtually all the Army, Navy and Marine aircraft parked on the five airfields of Wheeler, Hickam, Ford Island, Kaneohe Bay and Ewa. The sole cause for relief on the US side was that the carriers *Enterprise*, *Saratoga* and *Lexington* were not in harbor.

Until this attack, certainly the most effective sneak attack in the history of modern warfare, pathetically little was known of Japanese air power. At least, the up-to-date and detailed accounts from China had never been acted upon or disseminated, so that all three of the Pearl Harbor attack types were virtually unknown. To war-hardened Europeans they did not appear especially formidable. All three had radial engines of quite low power, giving modest performance. Though efficient stressed-skin machines, fitted with constant-speed propellers and flaps, they were all designs of the late 1930s and they looked supremely easy to shoot down. The D3A had a fixed undercarriage and resembled a lower-powered Ju 87 with smaller bombload of 250kg (551lbs), reaching a mere 322km/h (200mph) at sea level on a 1000hp engine and defended by a single machine gun in the rear cockpit. The B5N had only 840hp and was even slower, especially when burdened by an 800kg torpedo or a similar weight of bombs, and again had merely a single machine gun. The A6M2 had just

Right: *A US soldier looks on at scenes of destruction. It had taken almost four years of bitter fighting to bring the Japanese to book for Pearl Harbor.*

Right: A postwar replica of Mitsubishi's A6M2 Reisen (Zero) single-seat fighter.

Above: The Aichi D3A1 was the first Japanese aircraft of World War II to bomb US forces. It was code-named Val by the Allies.

940hp and could barely exceed 482km/h (300mph) at sea level, though at medium heights it could manage 534km/h (322mph). It had fair armament of two cannon and two machine guns, but on paper appeared out-classed by Allied machines.

Over the subsequent months the Japanese war machine spread over a bigger area of the Earth than had ever before been conquered by one country, and the speed of this vast conquest was awesome. Absolute command of the air was needed, and gained. The vulnerability of the D3A and B5N hardly mattered, because opposition was scattered and ineffectual. Allied fighters, a motley assortment from many countries flying under US, British, Australian, Dutch and Chinese command, were in most theaters completely routed. Hurricanes, P-40s,

Buffaloes, P-43As, CW-21s and Blenheim IFs were no match for the A6M, which could literally fly rings round them by virtue of its amazingly low wing-loading of 107kg/sq m (22lb/sq ft). As an example of the desperate measures adopted to try to dogfight these aircraft with some chance of winning, the 0.5in guns of RAF Buffaloes were replaced by small 0.303in caliber, with half the available amount of ammunition. The Buffaloes still had little chance.

On the Imperial Army side the main fighter was the Nakajima Ki-43, which could only just exceed 482km/h (300mph) at its best height on a 980hp engine, and had an arma-ment of only two machine guns. Entering service as recently as April 1941 it seemed on paper totally outdated, yet its amazing maneuverability – even greater than the bigger A6M — gave it an almost unbroken run of victories. Moreover, many of the Japanese pilots, especially in the Army, had gained great experience from years of fighting in China. Far from the Japanese being inferior, as had previously been thought, they temporarily swept the Allies from the sky. Typical of the results were the totals of 390 RAF and RAAF aircraft shot down against 92 Japanese during the campaign in Malaya and Singapore, the Japanese figure including machines hit by anti-aircraft fire.

There was just one Allied machine which, because of its toughness and large wing, did have at least a chance of evening the score. This was the Grumman F4F Wildcat, a tubby mid-wing carrier-based fighter powered by a Pratt & Whitney Twin Wasp or Wright Cyclone of 1200hp and with a patented main undercarriage retracting upwards into the

Left: *The Republic P-43 Lancer, a four-gun fighter with a turbocharged Pratt & Whitney R-1830 engine capable of 573km/h (356mph) in P-43A form, was both a development of the Seversky P-35 and precursor of the P-47 Thunderbolt.*

Below: *Sixty examples of the Seversky P-35A destined for Sweden in 1940 were requisitioned for the USAAF; 48 were sent to the Philippines in 1941 to bolster defenses, to little avail.*

Above: *The Nakajima Ki-43 Hayabusa (Allied code-name Oscar) was flown as a fighter and fighter-bomber in all areas of Japanese operations.*

fuselage. Usually armed with four (later six) guns, it could manage 500-523km/h (310-325mph) but had inferior climb and turn radius. Yet the margin was not great and until mid 1943 the Wildcat was almost the only Allied machine able to make any impression on the victorious Japanese air force in air-to-air combat.

The Wildcat was gradually improved, with a 1350hp Cyclone engine giving a speed of 534km/h (332mph). Far more important was Grumman's completely new F6F, first flown in June 1942 in the light of war experience.

Named Hellcat, this was powered by Pratt & Whitney's superb 18-cylinder R-2800 Double Wasp engine, giving 2000hp, and so it could be bigger, stronger and more heavily armed than the F4F, with six 0.5in guns and a speed of 605km/h (376mph). Hellcats poured from the Bethpage plant at such a rate that in two full years almost 11,000 entered service, and they completely reversed the tide of events in the Pacific sky. US Navy F6F units alone gained 4947 confirmed victories, and by 1944 many F6Fs were radar-equipped night fighters. Not least of their attributes was the

ability to carry a 907kg (2000lb) bombload.

The F6F had an able partner in the Chance Vought F4U Corsair. First flown years earlier, in May 1940, when it was the first fighter ever to exceed 644km/h (400mph), it took a long time to develop. Though used with success by Britain's Fleet Air Arm, it was rejected by the US Navy because of tricky deck-landing behavior and, until late in the war, it served mainly with the Marines. Distinguished by its cranked low wing (intended to give ground clearance for the giant propeller driven by the R-2800 engine), the F4U was much faster than the F6F and is considered by some the greatest piston-engined fighter of all time. Entering service in July 1942, it nudged 644km/h (400mph) and later far exceeded it, yet carried six machine guns or four cannon as well as heavy loads of bombs and rockets. Corsairs flew every kind of fighter, attack, night interception and reconnaissance mission, and did not go out of production until 1952.

By far the most important Allied attack bomber in the first two years of the Pacific War was the Douglas SBD Dauntless. Cast rather in the Japanese mold, with stressed-skin airframe, radial engine of modest power (a 1000hp Cyclone) and long 'greenhouse' canopy, the SBD was derived from a carrier-based bomber of 1935; series production

Left: *Progressive development of the A6M kept performance in line with Allied advances, the A6M5a (illustrated) possessing a level speed of about 565km/h (351mph), a fine diving speed, and with heavier-gauge skin and armament improvements.*

Above: *The only Allied fighter capable of dealing effectively with Japanese fighters during the early stages of the Pacific War was the US Navy's Grumman F4F Wildcat.*

Left: *Grumman's follow-on carrier fighter to the Wildcat was the F6F Hellcat.*

Above: *A Chance Vought F4U Corsair carrier-borne fighter-bomber, at the time of its appearance the most powerful naval fighter.*

Top right: *Douglas SBD Dauntless attack bombers photographed on board either USS* Enterprise *or* Yorktown *during the Battle of Midway.*

commenced in June 1940. Like all Navy machines it had forward-firing guns, but the one(s) that mattered was the 0.3in-caliber (later, a pair) aimed for defense from the rear cockpit. Under the belly could be carried a 1000lb bomb, while light weapons could be hung underwing. At about 402km/h (250mph) the SBD was not fast, but it was tough, easy to fly, could dive-bomb with precision, avoid AA fire even when heavily laden, and was generally loved by its crews. Although it was supposed to be replaced by the SB2C from early 1942, it stayed in pro-

duction until June 1944, the total of 5936 including A-24 versions for the Army.

The 'replacement' Curtiss SB2C Helldiver was troublesome, and never did succeed in being either popular or easy to fly. Powered by a 1700hp Cyclone 14 (R-2600), it could reach 451km/h (280mph) despite being much heavier than the SBD and carrying far more fuel. Bombload was the same, though the Helldiver carried it in an internal bay, and later versions also had wing racks for light bombs or rockets. First flown in November 1940, the SB2C needed over 880

Above: *Although virtually obsolete at the time of the US entry into World War II, the Douglas TBD-1 Devastator served on board both USS* Lexington *and* Yorktown *during the Battle of the Coral Sea.*

major design changes, some of them to assist standardization with the land-based A-25 version for the Army. Forward-firing armament comprised four machine guns or two cannon, and the gunner had an 0.5in gun for rear defense. Some 7200 eventually entered service, but it was November 1943 before the type got into action, during the fighting at Rabaul, New Britain.

The standard US Navy torpedo bomber, the Douglas TBD Devastator, was becoming obsolescent in December 1941, for it reached only 322km/h (200mph) on the power of an early 850hp Twin Wasp, and with a 1000lb torpedo slung externally the cruising speed was only 206km/h (128mph). Thus, the backseater with an 0.3in-caliber gun might have a lot to do, and from Pearl Harbor onwards the TBDs had a hard time, 35 out of 41 being shot down in a single engagement during the Battle of Midway in June 1942.

Thereafter the far superior Grumman TBF Avenger took over. First flown in August 1941, the TBF was a splendid machine in every way, with upper and lower rear gunners (the upper man having a precision-directed powered turret with an 0.5in gun) and a 1700hp R-2600 Cyclone engine, with a big internal bay for a short (22in) 2000lb torpedo or an equivalent load of bombs. Six went into action during the Midway battles; only one returned, and that was shot to pieces with one gunner dead and the other injured. This was not at all typical of later TBF actions, and the 9836 of these great machines produced did a fantastic job in many theaters, including defeating U-Boats in the Atlantic; 921 Avengers flew with the Fleet Air Arm and 63 with the RNZAF. Weighing up to 8278kg (18,250lbs), the Avenger was a hefty machine, but it handled well and was always very popular, continuing in service with many nations long after the end of the war.

Left: *The Grumman Avenger did a fantastic job as the US Navy's standard torpedo-bomber after its bad start during the Battle of Midway.*

Below: *The US Navy's first substantially-deployed twin-engined fighter-bomber was the Grumman F7F Tigercat, intended to serve on carriers of the new USS Midway class. The first prototype F7F flew at the end of 1943 and production aircraft were delivered from April of the following year, but few were in use by VJ-Day.*

Right: *Nakajima's successor to the B5N was the B6N Tenzan (Allied code-name Jill). This B6N2 is preserved in the United States.*

Its counterpart in the Imperial Navy was the B6N, Nakajima's straightforward B5N successor. Though it had an 1800hp Kasei engine, it is doubtful that the improved speed of up to 481km/h (299mph) did much for survivability in the face of F6Fs or the withering fire from warships from 1943 onwards; its load of one torpedo was likewise inadequate. Nakajima also produced a superficially similar machine, the C6N, for reconnaissance missions. This beautiful three-seater had a 1990hp Homare engine and could reach 610km/h (379mph) with enough fuel for a range of 5310km (3300 miles), but it served only in the war's final year.

The chief US Army fighters in the first year of the Pacific War were the Curtiss P-40 and Lockheed P-38. The P-40 Warhawk (also called Kittyhawk by British Commonwealth

Above: *The line of Grumman piston-engined fighters ended with the F8F Bearcat, a 677-719km/h (421-447mph) four-gun naval aircraft that was delivered from early 1945 but did not become operational before VJ-Day.*

Right: *The Curtiss P-40F was a much improved version of the Warhawk capable of 586km/h (364mph) on the power of its Packard V-1650-1 (Rolls-Royce Merlin) piston engine.*

forces) existed in various closely-related forms powered by the Allison V-1710 or Packard Merlin, both of about 1300hp. A typical maximum speed was 563km/h (350mph) and standard armament six machine guns, with provision in the attack role for a 500lb bomb under the fuselage and two of 250 or 500lb underwing. Based on the Hawk 75 of May 1935, the P-40 was naturally becoming somewhat dated, despite Curtiss' efforts at progressive improvement, and though it served well with the American Volunteer Group (later 14th Air Force) in China, it was hard-pressed to hold its own in the Pacific fighting.

Lockheed's P-38 Lightning was newer in concept, having been designed in 1938 to meet a US Army need for a 644km/h (400mph) fighter. The unusual layout put the pilot in a short central nacelle with concentrated armament of (usually) one 37mm cannon and four 0.5in machine guns. Two 1475hp Allison engines were mounted at the front of booms which not only carried the twin-fin tail but also the radiators (on the sides of each boom) and the turbosuperchargers recessed into the top. Thanks to this exhaust arrangement, the P-38 was

Below: *In 1943, the P-38H version of the Lightning appeared, with provision for 3200lbs of bombs in addition to guns.*

Above: *The Kawasaki Ki-45 Kai-C Toryu, code-named Nick.*

Left: *Republic P-47 Thunderbolts became operational in the Southwest region of the Pacific in mid 1943.*

Above: *Among the abandoned aircraft in this graveyard of Japanese warplanes can be seen an A6M Zero (foreground), a Mitsubishi J2M Raiden and two examples of the twin-engined Nakajima J1N1 Gekko.*

probably the quietest fighter ever built. Its greatest attribute was range, well demonstrated on 18 April 1943 when P-38Gs of the USAAF flew with great precision to intercept a G4M carrying Admiral Yamamoto, C-in-C of the Japanese fleet, almost 800km (500 miles) from their base on Guadalcanal. Though it could reach about 644km/h (400mph), and even carry a heavy bombload, the P-38 was at a slight disadvantage in a dogfight because of its size, and in particular its slow rate of roll resulting from its large wingspan of 15.85m (52ft).

The Japanese also produced some large twin-engined fighters. The main Army model was the Kawasaki Ki-45, first flown in January 1939. Though fitted with engines of only 1050hp, the Ki-45 had a useful speed of some 540km/h (336mph) and was beautiful to fly. There were many armament options,

including that of the Kai-C night fighter of spring 1944 with a 37mm gun firing ahead and two 20mm weapons mounted in the mid fuselage firing obliquely upwards. The main Navy twin-engined combat machine was the Nakajima J1N1, produced not only as an escort or night fighter but also as a reconnaissance aircraft. Powered by two 1130hp Sakae engines, the J1N1 first flew in May 1941 and had a maximum speed of about 529km/h (329mph). Again there were various arrangements of armament, but the J1N1-C Kai night fighter was unusual in having two pairs of cannon amidships, one pair firing obliquely upwards and the other obliquely downwards.

Among conventional single-engined fighters, the Army's Kawasaki Ki-44 Shoki (Demon) broke away from the previous tradition of agility at all cost and emphasized

Above: *The best Japanese Army fighter at the end of the war was the Kawasaki Ki-100, seen here in front of a preserved Me 262 of the Luftwaffe's JG7.*

speed, climb and firepower. Powered by a 1250hp engine, the prototype flew in August 1940 and was notable for its rather portly body and small wing and tail. Production Ki-44s had 1450 or even 2000hp engines and various armaments including guns of 7.7, 12.7, 20, 37 and 40mm caliber. The 40mm guns were odd in that each shell had its own fast-burning rocket charge ejecting through 12 small holes, no empty case having to be ejected. A typical speed for a Ki-44 was 605km/h (376mph), the same as an F6F, but for once the US fighter was usually able to turn tighter.

The corresponding Navy speed/firepower fighter was the Mitsubishi J2M Raiden (Thunderbolt), again noted for its portly body and small wing. Flown as late as March 1942, the prototype suffered from various snags but the J2M2 eventually got into production in early 1943 with a 1800hp Kasei engine giving a speed of 597km/h (371mph) – not a high figure for such a small, light and powerful fighter in which speed was a main objective. Again there were many armaments, typical being two 20mm cannon in the wing and two more either in the wing or in the fuselage. Mitsubishi never got very far with its planned A6M successor, the A7M Reppu (Hurricane) with a 2250hp engine and four or six cannon, so the old A6M had to continue in production in slightly improved forms, none of which really had the requisite engine power.

For the Army Kawasaki built several liquid-cooled engine fighters using a copy of the German DB 601A engine of 1175hp. The Ki-60 was flown in March 1941, but this was dropped in favour of the Ki-61, flown in December 1941 and first delivered in February 1943. Able to reach 592km/h (368mph), the Ki-61-Ib had two fuselage guns and two more in the wing, or (from mid 1943) two 20mm Mauser MG 151 cannon (the Japanese Ho-5 gun not yet being available). In summer 1944 the more powerful 1500hp Ha-140 engine intended for later Ki-61s was proving so unreliable that hundreds of airframes were lying about engineless. In a desperate emergency move, an example was converted to take the 1500hp Ha-112 radial, and the result was a startlingly good performer.

Far easier to fly, much more maneuverable and particularly reliable, the new machine was rushed into production as the Ki-100. Though not very fast at 580km/h (360mph), or heavily armed with two machine guns and two cannon, the Ki-100 was universally considered the best Army fighter at the end of the war. This was quite a tribute since the Army also had the superb Nakajima Ki-84 Hayate (Gale), first flown in March 1943 and soon in production with a 1900hp Ha-45 engine and able to reach 631km/h (392mph), as well as having long range and excellent handling qualities. Most had four cannon as well as racks for two 250kg bombs.

Below: A Kawanishi N1K2-J Shiden fighter (Allied code-named George 21), in the markings of the 343rd Kokutai. On one occasion in early 1945, a single Shiden brought down four US Hellcats of a formation of 12.

Left: A preserved example of the Kawasaki Ki-61 Hien.

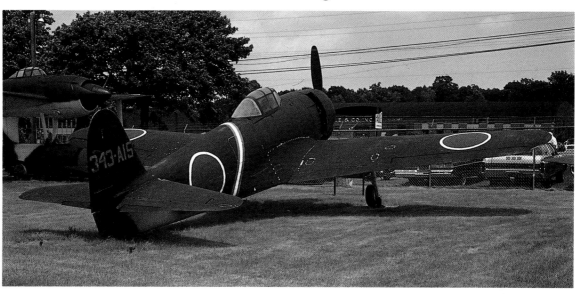

Below: Kawanishi developed the Shiden from the N1K Kyofu seaplane fighter (code-named Rex) which managed just over 480km/h (300mph) but, despite excellent qualities, was taken out of production after just 97 had been completed.

A roughly equivalent Navy fighter was the Kawanishi N1K Shiden (Violet Lightning). Odd in being a landplane conversion of a fighter seaplane, the N1K1 was able to reach 584km/h (363mph) on the power of its 1990hp Homare engine, and the usual armament comprised four cannon (sometimes with two fuselage-mounted machine guns as well). Though plagued by poor materials, and especially by a weak undercarriage, the N1K1-J version played a major role in staving off total eclipse of Japanese airpower from early 1944. Later models followed.

The Japanese had large numbers of simple tactical bombers of modest performance. First flown in 1937, the Kawasaki Ki-32 was still in wide use in 1941, with an 850hp liquid-cooled engine giving a speed of 423km/h (263mph). Slightly later in design, the Mitsubishi Ki-30 had a 950hp radial engine and reached an identical speed, bombload being 400kg (882lbs). The Tachikawa Ki-36 two-seater had only 510hp and a speed of 348km/h (216mph) and carried just two machine guns and various light bombs, but late in the war it was loaded with a 500kg bomb for suicide purposes.

For the Navy, the main carrier-based dive bomber to follow the D3A was the Yokosuka D4Y Suisei (Comet). First flown in 1940 with a 960hp DB 600G liquid-cooled engine, the D4Y went into production in early 1942 with a 1200hp Japanese copy of the DB 601, giving a speed of 552km/h (343mph), the 560kg (1234lb) bombload being housed internally. Many variants followed, including night fighters with an obliquely-installed cannon in the rear cockpit, all later versions having a more powerful 1560hp Kinsei radial engine.

The Yokosuka arsenal was also responsible for an outstandingly fast twin-engined machine in the class of the Ju 88, the P1Y Ginga (Milky Way). Powered by 1825hp Homare engines, this three-seater had a speed of 547km/h (340mph) and was produced with various armament schemes and served as a night fighter or as a bomber with 1000kg (2205lbs) of bombs or a torpedo.

The Navy's chief bombers were both products of Mitsubishi. The Ka-15 prototypes of 1935 led to the G3M, of which 1048 had been built by 1943. Powered by 1075 or 1300hp Kinsei engines, these five-seat twin-finned machines were noteworthy for their great range, many very accurate bombing missions being made as much as 2010km (1250 miles) from base. Most had a bomb or torpedo load of 800kg (1764lbs) and could reach a speed of 373km/h (232mph). Mitsubishi's

successor was the G4M, first flown in October 1939 to try to meet an Imperial Navy requirement for a bomber with a range of 2000 nautical miles while carrying an 800kg torpedo or equivalent bombload. The task demanded a four-engined bomber and the G4M, with two 1530hp Kasei engines, could not quite meet the demand even without the weight of self-sealing tanks, armor and other protection. As a result it was so vulnerable it was called 'the one shot lighter' by Allied fighter pilots, and though large numbers were built in steadily improved versions it never became a fully satisfactory machine. Early G4Ms did, however, collaborate with G3Ms in sinking the only two British capital ships in the Far East, HMS *Prince of Wales* and *Repulse*, on 10 December 1941, using both torpedoes and armor-piercing bombs.

The most numerous Army bomber was the Mitsubishi Ki-21, first flown in November 1936. From 1940 most were of the Ki-21-II type, with engine power increased from 850 to 1450hp, giving a maximum speed of just over 482km/h (300mph). This obsolescent but widely used machine carried a bombload of 1000kg (2205lbs), but was not well protected and relied mainly on hand-held machine guns for defense. Almost as numerous, with 1977 built compared with 2064, the

Kawasaki Ki-48 was quite a small four-seat bomber with 950 or 1150hp engines and a speed with the more powerful engines of 505km/h (314mph). Another of the Army bombers, the Nakajima Ki-49 Donryu (Storm Dragon) was slightly bigger and much heavier, and could reach 492km/h (306mph) on two 1450hp engines, carrying a bombload of 1000kg (2205lbs) and with defensive guns of 7.7, 12.7 and 20mm calibers. First flown in 1939, the Ki-49 entered service in late 1941, 819 of all versions being built. Easily the best of the Army bombers was the Mitsubishi Ki-67 Hiryu (Flying Dragon), first flown at the end of 1942. Powered by two 1900hp engines, this fine machine had a crew of six to eight yet still reached 537km/h (334mph) with a bombload of 800kg (1764lbs) and was protected by a cannon and four heavy machine guns.

There were no production four-engined bombers for either the Army or Navy, but the latter did have excellent large flying boats for reconnaissance and transport missions. Kawanishi's H6K, first flown in 1936, had four engines of 1000hp in most versions, giving a speed just over 322km/h (200mph). A total of 215 was built, some being unarmed civil transports. The same company's H8K, first flown in January 1941, is considered the

Above: *Nakajima's Ki-49-II, the main version of the Army Type 100 bomber.*

Opposite: *The 'H' version of the North American B-25 Mitchell was built for Pacific operations, carrying a 75mm cannon plus 14 machine guns.*

Below: *The chief Allied bomber of the Pacific War was the Consolidated B-24 Liberator.*

Below: *Of the various maritime patrol aircraft flown by the combatant nations, the most famous was undoubtedly the Consolidated PBY Catalina. A PBY-5A, capable of 288km/h (179mph) on the power of two 1200hp Twin Wasp engines, is seen here patrolling the Aleutian islands.*

best flying boat ever built for military purposes. Only 167 were made, most of them powered by four 1850hp Kasei engines giving a speed of 467km/h (290mph) and able to carry two torpedoes or 2000kg (4410lbs) of bombs while being heavily armed defensively with five machine guns.

In general, Japanese aircraft were more lightly constructed than those of the Allies, so that even with much less powerful engines they had good overall performance and often exceptional maneuverability. A typical example was the Mitsubishi Ki-46, originally

a reconnaissance aircraft but later developed as an interceptor and ground-attack fighter. First flown in 1939, it had twin engines of only 1050hp yet had a speed of 604km/h (375mph) and range of 2474km (1537 miles) or even 4000km (2485 miles) in later versions, as well as being extremely pleasant to fly. For most of the war the Ki-46 was almost immune from interception, and towards the end of the conflict it became an interceptor itself, being one of the few machines able to reach the high-flying American heavy bombers in 1945.

Right: The twin-engined Douglas B-18 Bolo and refined B-23 Dragon were both operated for a brief period at the start of US involvement in the war, neither type being used for bombing but undertaking patrols. The B-23 (illustrated) was the first US bomber with a tail-gun position.

Throughout the Pacific War the chief Allied heavy bomber was the Consolidated B-24 Liberator. First flown in December 1939, this was five years later in concept than the B-17 and was therefore far more complicated. Engines were four 1200hp Twin Wasps with turbosuperchargers giving good performance up to heights greater than 7620m (25,000ft), though the waist gunners at their open windows needed warm clothing! Most versions could reach 467km/h (290mph) and carry 3628kg (8000lbs) of bombs for more than 3220km (2000 miles), and a crew of 10 was needed to handle all the duties and man the defensive armament of at least 10 heavy machine guns. These great machines, which also served in transport versions carrying fuel 'over the Hump' into China, were partnered by numerous effective twin-engined medium bombers. The largest of these were the North American B-25 Mitchell and Martin B-26 Marauder.

Both flew in 1940 and were impressive machines defended by batteries of heavy machine guns including power-driven turrets, and both could carry bombloads of up to 1814kg (4000lbs) and reach speeds around 483km/h (300mph). They also served

in other theaters, but the Mitchell is remembered best for one of its first combat missions, a daring operation unlike anything for which it was designed. On 18 April 1942 the great US Army pilot Jimmy Doolittle led 16 B-25Bs off the pitching deck of the carrier USS *Hornet* (the B-25 had not been considered for shipboard operation). The formation flew at low level for 1290km (800 miles), then split up to drop bombs on Tokyo and other Japanese cities. The psychological effect was tremendous at a time when Japan seemed invincible and certainly immune to enemy attack.

The B-26 was slightly more powerful than the B-25, having 2000hp Double Wasps instead of 1700hp Cyclones, and was fractionally larger and heavier. The first B-26As, fitted to carry torpedoes externally, were deployed to Australia on the day after Pearl Harbor, and many later models served in the Pacific with a long-range fuel tank in the rear bomb bay, reducing bombload to 907kg (2000lbs). Aircraft such as these, together with Douglas A-20s and British and Australian-built Bristol Beaufighters, pounded the enemy with bombs, mines, rockets and gunfire around the clock.

Below: *A captured Yokosuka Ohka suicide aircraft. The Ohka's first successful kamikaze attack was mounted on 12 April 1945, when the destroyer USS Mannert L Abele was sunk.*

Right: *The nose art of B-29 Bockscar records the Nagasaki atom bomb attack.*

Throughout the war one major objective of the Allies had been to strike heavily at Japan itself, and this demanded a super long-range bomber. Such an aircraft had been started in 1938, and first flew on 21 September 1942 as the Boeing B-29 Superfortress, the biggest, heaviest and most complex aircraft of its day. Powered by four 2200hp Duplex Cyclones with twin turbosuperchargers, it had a wing loading of up to about 400kg/sq m (80lb/sq ft), more than double the usual for World War II aircraft. Moreover, the crew were sealed in pressurized cabins, and the formidable defensive firepower of one cannon and ten heavy machine guns was mounted in remotely-controlled turrets operated by gunners at special fuselage sighting stations and one in the tail.

B-29s were built by a great nationwide group with final assembly at Boeing, Bell and Martin. They flew their first combat mission in June 1944, the crews gradually learning how to achieve a range of 5230km (3250 miles) with a 4536kg (10,000lb) bombload, cruising at up to 467km/h (290mph) at heights over 9150m (30,000ft). A mighty

Below: *Boeing B-29 missions were initially flown against Japanese targets from China and India (as shown).*

Far right: *The crew of B-29 Dina Might relax before a mission.*

armada was swiftly created, based chiefly on airfields in the newly-captured Marianas, and by spring 1945 formations of up to 500 were reducing Japan's cities to rubble and ashes. From 9 March 1945 the attacks were made by night from quite low level, using incendiaries; the results were devastating.

Japan's only answer was to step up 'kamikaze' suicide operations in which pilots deliberately crashed bomb-laden aircraft into Allied shipping. All kinds of aircraft were used for such missions, often carrying far more than the usual bombload, but several aircraft were specially built. The most significant of these was the Yokosuka MXY-7 Ohka (Cherry Blossom), a manned missile carried under a G4M and released near the target. The pilot was to glide towards the target and then fire a powerful three-barrel rocket engine so that the final dive reached a speed close to 966km/h (600mph). Though 852 Ohkas were built, few hit their targets, mainly because the parent bombers were so vulnerable to attack before the Ohkas could be launched.

On 6 August 1945 a specially equipped B-29 named *Enola Gay* dropped a 12½-kiloton yield atomic weapon on the city of Hiroshima. Another B-29, *Bock's Car*, dropped a different type of atomic bomb on the city of Nagasaki on 9 August, and on 14 August 754 B-29s (escorted by 169 fighters) of the 20th Army Air Force attacked Japan with conventional weapons: the latter was the final USAAF wartime mission. Japan surrendered to the Allies without an invasion that would have cost many thousands of lives. On 19 August two G4Ms carried the Japanese surrender delegation to Ie Shima, and on 2 September the Japanese surrender documents were signed on board the battleship USS *Missouri* at anchor in Tokyo Bay. World War II was over.

INDEX

ACKNOWLEDGEMENTS

The photographs are from the author's collection,
with the exception of those listed below:

Gordon Bain 34
Bell Helicopter Textron 102
Bison Picture Library 1, 7, 8, 9, 12-3, 16 (top), 17,
20, 21, 22-3, 26-7, 36-7, 38, 44 (both), 47 (lower),
51, 55, 56-7, 73, 76-7 (above), 82, 93, 94, 95,
104, 105, 107, 108, 109, 110 (both), 114, 116-7,
120, 121 (both), 130-1, 133 (above), 137, 145
(below), 150-1, 152-3
Boeing 76-7, 78-9, 79, 80-1, 156, 156-7, 157
Charles E Brown 25
Candid Aero-Files 98, 132 (below), 146 (above)
McDonnell Douglas 84-5
Grumman Aerospace Corporation 135 (both), 138-
9, 139, 140
Bill Hobson/Michael J H Taylor 11, 123
Imperial War Museum 4-5, 40-1, 67, 68-9, 96-7,
109, 114-5, 119, 122
Kawasaki Heavy Industries 145 (above)
Lockheed-California 28-9, 30-1, 72-3, 102-3, 142-3
Messerschmitt—Bölkow-Blohm GmbH 18-9, 98-9
Musée de l'Air 32-3
Matthew Nathan 106
Northrop 91
Piaggio 112-3
RAF Museum, Hendon 42-3, 48-9, 50, 52-3, 61
(upper), 64-5, 65 (top, center), 66 (both), 69, 70
(top, bottom) 74, 75 (above), 84, 85, 89 (below),
106 (above)
Bob Snyder 132 (above), 133 (below), 140-1
(above), 146 (below), 147 (both)
Stato Maggiore Aeronautica 111 (both)
US Air Force 2-3, 58-9, 82-3, 83, 88-9, 89 (above),
90-1, 92-3, 101 (below), 140-1 (below), 144, 153
Vought Corporation 136-7